ABOUT THIS BOOK

Chapter 1.....The D.R.I.V.E.R. System--An explanation of the six elements of super test taking.

Chapter 2.....D is for DIET (NUTRITION)--Discover how diet effects learning and energy. Learn what foods to avoid on the day of a test and what foods will give you added energy and more mental power.

Chapter 3.....R is for RELAXATION--Learn all about Brain States and physical exercises that will allow for immediate relaxation and provide the ability to perform in a peak manner under pressure.

Chapter 4.....I is for INDIVIDUALITY--Discover ways to determine how we are smart and how to use this information to increase our individual learning power.

Chapter 5.....V is for VISUALIZING CONFIDENCE-- Discover the amazing world of visualization and how to use this goal achieving skill to build confidence and increase test scores.

Chapter 6.....E is for ENERGY STATES--Explore strategies for using humor, music, stretching, and physical exercises to "wake-up" the brain for peak performance.

Chapter 7.....R is for REMEMBER--Learn techniques for making memory a breeze. Discover strategies for learning, encoding and recalling information almost automatically.

TABLE OF CONTENTS

PREFACE

What is so terrible that it can cause children to lay awake through sleepless nights tossing and turning with images of failure and self-contempt in their thoughts? What could cause them to shake with fear and anxiety, to sweat profusely, and to breathe sporadically while throwing eating habits and digestion into disarray? What could psychosomatically produce physical ailments such at stomach cramps, loose bowel movements, headaches, irritability and frayed nerves? What is it that eats away at self-esteem and makes children doubt their ability and feel inadequate? What could create such turmoil in our families and society?

In Ohio and New York, the culprit is called The Proficiency Test. In Michigan, it is known as the MEAP (Michigan Education Assessment Program). In California, it's called the STAR Program. And in Indiana, it goes by the name ISTEP+. Virginians call it SOL or the Standard of Learning while in West Virginia, it is known as SET 9. It has many names, but the general term is Standardized Testing and its effects are far reaching.

State governments have passed laws mandating that students pass these tests but offer few suggestions for improved performance. Governors and Mayors have preached the benefits of the tests and in the same breath have threatened students with non-graduation, summer school, tutors, and special programs. Communities have held town meetings and hired specialists and guest speakers to discuss alternatives and find solutions. Parents blame the teachers, teachers blame the administrators, administrators blame the government and students blame themselves all in one vicious circle.

Teachers and administrators across the country fear for their careers if the students in their schools cannot pass these tests. Teachers in some areas admit to "teaching to the test", spending the majority of class time learning, practicing, and drilling very specifically towards raising standardized test scores while never touching upon other necessary life skills. In other areas, teachers and administrators have admitted to, or have been caught, helping students to cheat on the tests in order to save their educational careers.

Parents have screamed, punished, yelled, hired tutors, withheld allowances, threatened, pleaded, begged, coerced, and much more in order to urge their children to study hard and pass these mandatory tests. Some parents have given up. Some have told their kids they are worthless or, worse yet, stupid or dumb.

Some kids have given up, wondering "what's the use". Others have quit their education or contemplated suicide or simply "dropped out". Some of these children will never know that they were born *geniuses*.

The pressure is ruthless. Particularly when we don't arm our students with the tools and techniques to handle such pressure. This book was produced to do just that. To arm students and teachers with methods and techniques that will allow for peak performance under pressure in the classroom, specifically during test taking situations.

Some of the techniques are taken from the world of sport. Can you believe that the same techniques that allow Tiger Woods to sink a putt or Michael Jordon to make a foul shot can help a student learn to read faster, with more comprehension and recall? Or that a method used by Joe Montana to access the peak-performance state could possibly double the amount of learning that occurs during a study session?

Other techniques are shared from the business arena. Some methods learned by sales people to size up their clients can actually help students spell better. Tools used by CEOs for motivation can also be implemented in the classroom to raise confidence and expectations.

Many of the techniques are based upon the growing body of knowledge in the area of neuroscience and brain based learning that teaches us how the brain likes to learn and how to use this amazing research to increase the power of our study skills, memory, recall, time-management, and environment.

Many of the suggestions are common sense. Others are obscure morsels of knowledge or the latest discoveries in mind-body techniques that can short cut our path to better learning and peak performance under pressure.

Read on and in Chapter One discover the elements of the **D.R.I.V.E.R.** System that will allow you to take control over your performance states and learn how to overcome the obstacles of pressure and self doubt in order to become an awesome test taker.

CHAPTER 1

The D.R.I.V.E.R. System

*T*he **DRIVER** System was created to combine six crucial elements of peak performance and adapt them to performing in a peak manner under pressure—specifically in the area of test taking. The formula revealed in this book will work extremely well for elevating test scores, but can also be used to enhance performance in other areas like sports, business and personal well being.

This chapter will serve as an overview of this formula, explaining each facet of the acronym while giving some basic background of its particular relation to peak performance.

The "**D**" stands for **DIET** or Nutrition. It has long been established that what we eat can affect how we feel. New research emphatically indicates that the effect of diet goes way beyond that. Diet can actually influence which areas of the brain are active at any certain time. It can also stifle mind-body communication and switch our moods and emotional states, causing hyperkinetic behavior, mental confusion, anxiety, nervousness and other negative performance behaviors. Startling new research at Cornell University suggests that nutrition can actually affect our offspring by controlling gene expression. This dramatic new research has far reaching implications and adds to the mountains of modern research that reinforces what mothers

have known for centuries as they scolded their children and implored them to
"WATCH WHAT YOU EAT"! [1]

The **"R"** stands for **RELAXATION**. It has long been determined that the relaxed performer in most cases has a better chance of performing at a higher level no matter what the endeavor. However, most students and younger athletes are never shown relaxation techniques or educated about the benefits associated with them. The **DRIVER** technique covers this subject in great detail.

The **"I"** stands for **INDIVIDUALITY** or Style. Every human being has their individual learning style and specific areas of intelligence. Just like we all have different likes and dislikes. Just because our friends can grasp material by using certain methods doesn't mean we'll be able to learn using the same methods. Discover your individual style and the power that comes with it.

The **"V"** stands for **VISUALIZING CONFI-DENCE**. What we believe about ourselves along with our expectations about life usually have a way of coming true. Learn how to develop a powerful belief system about learning. Learn how to visualize becoming a peak performer and how to turn that visualization into your reality.

15

The **"E"** symbolizes **ENERGY AND BRAIN STATES**. Humans are capable of creating specific energy states that allow for peak performance in any situation. Also, new research indicates that we are able to switch and control these brain states to take advantage of the ones that work best for us. Learn all about this amazing brain technology while learning how to activate and "turn on" the many "brain switches" located on our bodies and found in our environment.

And at last, the **"R"** stands for **REMEMBER**. There have been countless techniques discovered for improving memory. They range from listening to certain types of music to ingesting herbs containing special memory enhancement properties. The **DRIVER** method contains specific memory techniques that will not only allow for added recall at test time, but also provide more learning to take place during the study session. Every student comes equipped with an amazing ability to remember, but how to access the memories can sometimes be a problem. Combining new research concerning brain based learning techniques along with exciting discoveries about the mind/body connection can help anyone develop a super memory.

After reading about the **DRIVER** method in chapters 2 through 7, you will discover two additional chapters. Chapter 8 contains important research that will help you construct an awesome, brain-friendly learning room right in your own home. And Chapter 9 consists of a checklist and suggestions for peak performance before and during the test that will allow you to put to use all the knowledge you've just acquired. **By reading all the chapters in this book, you will become an awesome test taker!**

Go For It!!

CHAPTER 2

D for DIET
(NUTRITION)

$\mathcal{H}$uman beings can sometimes be a puzzle. For instance, most people know through common sense that certain foods are not good for them, hold no nutritional value, and affect the way they think and perform. *BUT THEY EAT THEM ANY-WAY!!*

We all know that food provides fuel in order for the body and brain to work properly. Current research also *proves* that what we eat can change the chemical balance of the brain, resulting in swift changes of emotional states, mood swings, energy fluctuations, and the inability to think clearly and access the peak performance state.

This chapter will not deal in depth with all the technical explanations of how and why certain foods affect our bodies and minds. Most students and parents could care less about the "*how*" and "*why*", but definitely are concerned about the "*what*". At my seminars people always say, "I really don't have time for all this information. Please just *TELL ME WHAT TO EAT*".

So I tell them and I can back up everything I say with the latest research. But no one seems to listen. If they did they wouldn't be eating donuts and coffee for breakfast or candy bars for afternoon snacks or sugar water sodas with potato chips in

the evening. Consistent superior mental performance is the direct result of a consistent high quality energy supply. Therefore, we will concentrate
on what and when to eat certain foods rather than
lengthy discussions on why they work or don't
work and how they change the chemical balance of
the brain and blood supply.

Keep in mind that the most important aspect of
developing peak performance eating habits is to
insure that the nervous system has an adequate
supply of glucose throughout the day. Without that
continuous supply, concentration and focus are
almost impossible and mental fatigue will surely
develop. With that understanding, let's go for it.

First and foremost, **NEVER GO WITHOUT
BREAKFAST**. Your energy demands begin to rise
the minute you awaken and without proper fuel
your performance system begins to labor and ulti-
mately shut down. The correct fuel at this crucial
meal can sometimes determine how your whole day
will turn out.

To be alert and have energy on the day of the
test, avoid refined or simple carbohydrates, like
sugar, when planning breakfast. These are ingested
into the blood too quickly and produce chemicals
that can reduce the flow of energy to the brain.
Complex carbohydrates like whole grains and fresh

fruit and vegetables provide a steadier supply of glucose to the brain.

To keep the supply of glucose steady, it's important that digestion occurs slowly and continuously. Therefore, most performance consultants suggest grazing throughout the day and partaking in 5 or 6 light meals rather than 3 large meals per day.

On test day make sure to eat an energy-producing snack at 10:00 or 10:30 in the morning. This snack should be friendly to the brain and easy to digest. It's important to start this snack with a food high in protein like cheese, meat, peanuts or milk. The reason for this is carbohydrates will produce certain amino acids (tryptophan) that can trigger the brain to produce large amounts of serotonin causing a relaxed feeling. If protein gets into the body first, it delivers an amino acid called tyrosine causing the brain to produce the neurotransmitters dopamine and norepinephrine which are alertness chemicals keeping you mentally alert. Thinking quickly and accurately while allowing the brain to handle the challenges and problem solving on the test. [1]

Always remember that what gets into the body first establishes dominance. Eat carbohydrates for relaxation and eat protein for mental alertness. The quicker you want to experience the relaxation or alertness effect, the less fat should be ingested with the meal. Eating fat will slow the rate of absorption into the system because it is hard to digest. This also slows mental processes because more blood and oxygen in the body is sent to the stomach for digestion purposes and, therefore, less oxygen is sent to the brain. [2]

A good list of protein foods for your energy snack include:
  · Shellfish
  · Fish
  · Chicken (without skin)
  · Veal
  · Low fat cottage cheese
  · Skimmed or low-fat milk
  · Low-fat yogurt
  · Dried peas and beans
  · Lentils
  · Soy Nuts
  · Egg whites are excellent for the brain

Also include fruits like peaches, apples, oranges and bananas for your snack. Leafy green vegetables and bright colored veggies like lettuce, spinach, broccoli, carrots and beets are recommended. [3]

Fat neither increases or decreases production of mind altering or mood modifying chemicals and should be included sparingly at any meal. The most important reason for this is that high fat foods take so long to digest. The longer digestion takes, the more blood and oxygen are diverted to the intestinal tract. Scientists have discovered that when blood is diverted down to the stomach and intestines rather than to the brain, mental energy and acuity tend to diminish. Avoid these breakfast foods when you need powerful mental skills:

- Sausage
- Bacon
- French fries or greasy home fries and hash-browned potatoes
- Cream cheese
- Butter
- Fast-food combos like sausage-and-egg croissant, ham and cheese   croissants, and English muffins topped with cheese, egg, and sausage
- Pastries such as donuts, coffee cake, sweet rolls, and Danishes. [4]

If you must have these foods, or if you find yourself at a place that doesn't serves good things to eat, then order a plain donut instead of one that is iced, glazed or chocolate filled. Ask for toast, a bagel or a bran muffin and don't use the cream cheese or butter. If you want an egg, have it poached, soft boiled or scrambled with very little butter rather than fried. Make intelligent choices.

Sometimes the response desired from our diet will be one of calmness with a focused state of mind. This can be achieved by eating the following grains and starches:

- Bread
- Pasta
- Potatoes
- Rice
- Crackers
- Muffins
- Bagels

Since each person is different and our bodies react in unique ways to the types of foods we eat, I always suggest keeping an eating journal. Test yourself one day with a carbohydrate breakfast and then the next day with a protein breakfast. Then possibly combine the two. Always keep track of the order in which the foods are taken into the body. Notice the state of mind and body before the meal and after the meal by taking good notes. You'll soon be able to develop power breakfasts, snacks, lunches and dinners for your specific digestive system and metabolism.

Always drink at least 8 glasses of water per day. The brain is over 80% water and loss of this precious fluid results in lower quality physical and mental performance. In the days before a test or athletic contest, be sure to drink plenty of water at every opportunity to avoid the detrimental effects of dehydration. Most nutritionists estimate that over 75% of students arrive to school dehydrated every day. This means they are already at a tremendous disadvantage for developing the mental acuity needed for power test taking. The average student's diet consists of candy bars containing caffeine, potato chips, soda and other dehydrating ingredients. Certain chemicals contained in these foods, called diuretics, dehydrate the body and can impair the learning process. These include alcohol and caffeine found in coffee, tea, carbonated beverages and chocolate. Avoid these chemicals and **drink plenty of water.**

It is crucial to avoid pop or soda at all costs. This colored sugar water is not only detrimental to physical performance, but the influence it has upon the delicate chemical balance in the brain is alarming. Let's explore the harmful ingredients found in most soft drinks. The common components of soda are phosphoric acid, caffeine, sugar or aspartame, caramel coloring, and aluminum. Why is there no poison label on most of these soda products?

Phosphoric acid is the same stuff used to get rust off cars or to clean deposited minerals in the shower. The container warns that the acid is "harmful if swallowed". A tooth will dissolve in it-

- can you imagine how many cavities can be prevented from limiting soda intake? Phosphoric acid causes the body to use up its alkaline minerals causing a shortage in neutral compounds like calcium. New studies indicate that abusing soft drinks at an early age can cause weakening of the joints and bones along with osteoporosis when we become older. This acid can also cause bloating and flatulence and increase the occurrence of digestive disorders and ulcers.

Caffeine does stimulate mental alertness and lessens fatigue, but it also stimulates the central nervous system. Caffeine also constricts the cerebral arteries while causing rapid heartbeat, high blood pressure, and excessive excretion of urine. **It is also addictive**! When regular users are deprived of their daily consumption of caffeine, the results are mental sluggishness, unclear thinking, depression, mood swings, and dull headaches.

A 12-ounce can of soda contains 33 grams or 11 teaspoons of sugar. In the United States, about 50% of all carbohydrates eaten are sugar. The average adult eats 150 pounds of sugar each year, but a teenager ingests over 300 pounds per year! And the trend rises each year. Food manufacturers are currently taking fat out of foods and adding sugar to deceptively advertise their foods as "fat-free". Not counting all the physical dangers of

sugar like more tooth decay, lower immune function, and the body's conversion of sugar to fat,
another powerful reason for limiting consumption is
the affect of sugar on the brain and learning. In
studies done at the National Institute of Mental
Health, high sugar diets limited student's attention
spans, their ability to focus and concentrate, and
their activity levels. Researchers already know that
sugar affects behavior and sparks learning disabilities in children. It makes them lethargic and tired,
creates a barrier in communication between the
body and brain, and causes an inability to think
clearly and solve problems accurately. All sugar
does is starve your brain because it robs the brain
and body of all water-soluble vitamins and minerals. When your child has sugar donuts or sugar
coated cereal before school, his blood sugar level
drops resulting in forgetfulness, lack of oxygen to
the brain, and the inability to concentrate. Refined
sugar is particularly insidious since it produces a
type of addiction as severe as any drug addiction.

** Researchers at the National Institute of
Mental Health found that the mentally crippling
effects of sugar were multiplied when the sugar was
eaten with carbohydrates. However, when small
amounts of sugar were eaten with protein the sugar
became beneficial to the brain and to learning.
Apparently, sugar is utilized differently when car-
ried into the body with protein. Before a test or

when learning new material, it may actually be helpful to eat protein with a small amount of sugar!

If you thought that by drinking diet soda you were eating better, than think again! One additive found in most diet soda is aspartame. Aspartame is not only found in pop, but is an ingredient of NutraSweet™. NutraSweet™ is used in candy bars, cookies and almost everything as a way to replace sugar. When digested it breaks down into three chemicals: aspartic acid, phenylalanine and methanol.

Aspartic acid can cause serious neurological disorders. It can overstimulate neurons to such an extent that sensitive neurons are slowly destroyed before behavioral symptoms are even noticed. In other words, brain cells are killed before there is any indication of a problem existing.

Phenylalanine decreases serotonin levels leading to emotional disorders, depression and poor quality sleep. By the way, Phenylalanine is contained in many diet colas (check out the first ingredient in Pepsi One™) and it can actually make a person gain weight!! The American Cancer Society has found that replacing sugar with NutraSweet™ or Equal™ can actually make you put on the pounds. The reason is that the phenylalanine in these compounds affects the part of the brain that makes you feel full. The result is that more will be eaten at the meal than would have with another beverage and that people who take these chemicals get intense sugar cravings and in the end—EAT MORE SUGAR! In addition, more studies show that NutraSweet™ can lead to hypothyroidism, which usually causes tremendous weight gain. The truth is that diet sodas are far worse for the brain and performance than regular sodas, but both are horrendous for our health.

** Instead of these beverages, try some sparkling water or purified tap water. You can flavor them with a wedge of lime or lemon or a touch of orange juice. Your brain and body will thank you.

Aspartame also breaks down into methanol. Methanol is a poison that is metabolized by the liver into formaldehyde (a deadly neurotoxin, carcinogen, mutagen and teratogen causing birth defects) and formic acid. Methanol is a cumulative poison whose symptoms include headaches, shooting pains, memory lapses and blurred vision. Just what you want in your system on test day!!

Some new studies will reveal that aspartame is actually good for you and should be included more in your diet. **It's very important you check out who pays for these studies.** All of these positive studies were funded with millions of dollars donated by the largest manufacturers of this sugar water. That's like Mike Tyson doing a study on anger control. Just be aware of the following:

- Airline pilots are requested to not drink aspartame before a long flight.

- Pregnant women are asked by their doctors to never ingest foods containing aspartame during the pregnancy.

- Doctors and psychologists suggest that children with learning disabilities, particularly ADD and ADHD, should NEVER eat anything containing aspartame.

Other food additives can be harmful to the brain, memory, and learning. Some of the prominent food additives to avoid are MSG and food coloring.

MSG is in almost everything. It is used to enhance flavor, however, has no flavor of its own and virtually no nutritional value. It doesn't actually make the food taste better, but it produces a flavor-enhancing effect by changing the way your brain perceives the taste! In other words, MSG doesn't change the food you eat, *IT CHANGES YOU!* The government says that MSG in its pure form must be labeled, but food manufacturers are now adding enormous amounts of MSG to our food under devious and difficult names like Hydrolyzed Protein and Sodium Caseinate. Ingestion of MSG is known to produce a variety of adverse reactions in all parts of the body including disorders of the Muscular, Neurological, Urological, Respiratory, and Gastrointestinal systems. Heart malfunctions, skin conditions, visual impairment, and circulatory problems are also common. Symptoms include headaches, vomiting, diarrhea, asthma attacks, anxiety attacks, heart palpitations, balance difficulties, mental confusion, mood swings, runny nose, behavioral disorders, and much more.

For more information on MSG, read the book **In Bad Taste: The MSG Syndrome** by George R. Schwartz, M.D. or call 800-232-8674.

The food coloring in soda can have the effect of "scattering" our thinking and making it hard to focus and concentrate on a specific task or problem. **Never drink colored sodas or powdered sweet drinks** when you need to rely on mental acuity. In other words, avoid these liquids before test taking sessions or athletic contests, board meetings, sales calls, classroom learning, budget meetings, brain storming sessions, drama productions, band or concert recitals, long drives, debates, study dates, etc. **GET THE PICTURE?** For a healthy life, avoid these colored sugar water drinks commonly called soda or soft drinks.

By the way, the aluminum found in the sodas is there because the phosphoric acid leaches this mineral from the can. There is enough aluminum in these drinks to be considered a "toxic amount". Aluminum is deposited in the brain and bone tissue and has a cumulative property. Aluminum given to rats resulted in the formation of neurofibrillary tangles in the brain tissue—the same type of lesion seen in the brains of individuals who suffer Alzheimer's disease.

If you take the time to notice exactly what students are eating, even during the school day, you won't be surprised at the changes in behavior, attitude, and learning. One of the largest studies ever conducted showing how significantly diet affects learning took place in 803 of the New York City Public Schools in 1979-1983. One million school children were involved in the study based upon the "Feingold" diet. During a four-year period, the schools eliminated artificial colors, artificial flavors, and preservatives like BHA and BHT. They also reduced the amount of sugar in the cafeterias' food. To assess their learning progress, the children took the California Achievement Test the three years before and the four years during the study. [5]

The results were spectacular! The International

Journal of Biosocial Research published the study and the authors wrote, "In short, New York City Public Schools raised their mean national academic performance percentile rating from 39.2% to 54.9% in four years, with the gains occurring in the first, second and fourth years (precisely when the dietary improvements were made)." [6]

What is also interesting is the fact that before the dietary changes, 12.4% of the one million student sample were performing two or more years below grade level. At the end of the study, that rate had dropped to 4.9%. Astounding! [7]

For more information on the Feingold Diet, contact the Feingold Association at 800-321-3287.

More information on diet and its relation to performance read **Eat To Win** by Dr. Robert Haas, **Managing Your Mind & Mood Through Food** by Judith J. Wurtman, Ph.D., and **Fit or Fat** by Covert Bailey. Covert Bailey has a fantastic audio program available through Nightengale Conant (1-800-323-5552) called **Living Smart, Staying Healthy** that cuts through the health myths and fads in a common sense and entertaining manner. **The A.D.D. and A.D.H.D. Diet** by Rachel Bell and Dr. Howard Peiper.

To give you an idea of a performance enhancing diet, the following is an excerpt from the workbook included with my audio program entitled **"Turning Slumps Into Streaks"**. This program contains an actual menu for athletes and students to implement for peak performance. **"Turning Slumps Into Streaks"** can be ordered by calling 419-424-3910 or accessing our web site at www.thewinnersedge.cc

The following are excerpts from the workbook "Turning Slumps Into Streaks" by Bruce Boguski

FOR TRAVELING ATHLETES, STUDENTS AND SALES PROFESSIONALS

At restaurants order pancakes, waffles, whole wheat French toast, bagels, muffins, cereal, fruit or juices. Carry fresh apples or oranges and small containers of juice or water

Emphasize the bread in sandwiches, not the filling. Avoid burgers, fried fish, fried chicken and french fries. You'll get more carbos by sticking to sandwiches, baked potatoes and chili. Try soup with crackers, bread or muffins for a low-fat, high carbo meal. Choose juice or skim milk rather than soft drinks.

Try restaurants that offer Italian foods. Request thick crust pizza with less sausage and pepperoni.

TRAVEL SNACK HINTS

Breads, bagels and muffins, crackers and pretzels. Fig Newtons, oatmeal and raisin cookies. Fruit juices or tomato juice or V-8 juice. Individual boxes of breakfast cereal, dried fruits, fresh fruits and vegetables.

BREAKFAST HINTS

Don't miss breakfast – you need to feed your muscles and your brain. Stay away from fatty substances they are too hard to digest and excess fat is contained. Eat high in fiber, low in sugar foods. A whole fruit is better than concentrated juice.

Drink 8 glasses of water a day. The brain is over 85% water. Over 60% of the body mass is water. A 3 % water loss hinders muscle contraction by 30 %, causing drastic performance loss.

Stay away from coffee, tea or hot chocolate.
They are stimulants and could upset your reaction
time and they will dehydrate you.

No chocolate bars, soft drinks or sweets right
before your performance. They rob you of your
water supply and a prolonged low follows a sugar
high.

Don't skip meals – you need to put energy into
your body all day. Eat smaller meals but eat them
more often.

If you need to actually see what a good performance meal would be like, here are some sample
menus.

BREAKFAST

Apple juice, oatmeal, skim milk, banana, and whole
wheat toast

(or)

Orange juice, pancakes with very little syrup and
low-fat yogurt

(or)

Raisin Bran, skim milk, muffins or toast and
fresh fruit

LUNCH

Large chicken sandwich on whole wheat bread, low-fat yogurt, fresh vegetable strips, fresh fruit and skim milk.

(or)

Sliced turkey, baked potato, peas and 2 slices of whole wheat bread

DINNER

Minestrone soup, spaghetti with meat sauce, parmesan cheese, Italian bread, skim milk and fresh fruit.

(or)

Lean roast beef, brown rice, corn bread, or rolls, skim milk and frozen yogurt

Eric Jensen, author of The Great Memory Book, lists the following ten foods for helping to develop a super memory:

1. Fish, especially cold water variety.
2. Eggs are great for the brain.
3. Soybeans. Soy nuts are a fantastic mid morning snack for alertness.
4. Lean Beef. Always cut the fat for more energy and better health.
5. Chicken Livers. It takes a special palette, but these livers are all brain food.
6. Whole Wheat. Stay away from white foods like sugar, flour, and salt.
7. Chicken. Good protein source.
8. Bananas. Carry them with you and eat anywhere.
9. Low Fat Diary Products. Develop a taste for skim milk early in life.
10. Avocados. Make your own special salsa.

Add the above foods to your already healthy diet for fantastic results. [8]

Certain nutrients have been shown to not only increase learning, but can also raise the IQ!! Dr. Vernon Mark, President of Boston's Center for Memory Impairment and Neuro-Behavior Disorders, notes that the recommended dietary allowances for good nutrition found on product labels were established by analyzing *disease states* and were not developed for optimal mental functioning. Therefore, many nutritionists, health care professionals, and scientists suggest the addition of nutritional supplements to a healthy well-balanced diet. The addition of the B vitamins will aid in the function of the immune system and impact mental energy. Vitamin C is also important for the role it plays in the in the production of certain memory neurotransmitters.

A study of British school children found that by taking a simple multi-vitamin formula over an eight month period of time increased nonverbal IQ by almost 10 points. Also noted in another study was that those students who had the lowest intake vitamin C and B-complex vitamins consistently scored lower on memory tests. Recent research on Vitamin A has revealed that its antioxidant properties can contribute to long term learning. And Vitamin E's ability to supply oxygen can aid in learning and memory.

New research on minerals and the effect they have on the brain suggest that boron, zinc, and magnesium are especially helpful in memory function. Magnesium shortages have been shown to cloud memory by slowing blood circulation while zinc deficiencies have been linked to mental confusion. Taking these minerals along with manganese, iron, calcium, iron and selenium can improve alertness, increase memory, and help in learning new material. When we take into account the hundreds of **"empty calories"** consumed by children every day, taking supplements can only aid in the health and learning processes of today's student.

CHAPTER 3

R is for
RELAXATION

$\mathcal{M}$ost researchers will agree the most influential element that effects how a student will perform on standardized tests is **ANXIETY**. They will also agree that, in most cases, the student who is relaxed will outperform the student that is uptight and nervous. Therefore, a student's ability to cope with pressure directly influences his or her test taking ability. The problem is that our school systems fail to teach the students how to handle pressure. There are no courses on relaxation. Proper breathing and stretching methods are not taught, but we still expect pupils to relax and perform at an optimal level while under intense pressure.

And, **WOW**, the pressure associated with these tests is enormous. Weeks before the tests gloomy headlines appear in the newspapers. The articles are filled with anecdotes and information predicting that students from certain backgrounds and geographical areas are not going to score well on standardized tests. Other articles warn teachers about losing their jobs if scores drop or if too little improvement occurs. They warn schools about losing crucial funding if scores fall below the established guidelines. And they threaten students with being held back or denied graduation unless their scores are above the benchmark. The tales of gloom and doom are horrific! The pressure is so great that students and teachers across the country have been caught cheating or altering scores just to make muster.

The good news is that stretching, breathing, and visualization techniques exist that can be easily taught and are relatively simple to implement into almost any ones testing strategy. These techniques can immediately produce a relaxed state and not only promote peak performance in test-taking ability, but also in sports and business. How many times have you heard a coach scream at the top of his or her lungs, "JUST RELAX" or a teacher tell his class, "Just relax and this will be easy"? In most cases, this is the closest that many students ever get to instruction on the proper methods used for relaxation.

In order to use relaxation techniques effectively, some background is necessary. As science progressed, a device called an Electroencephalogram or EEG was invented to measure the electrical activity that occurs in the brain. It was discovered that at any given moment, every thought and every feeling had a corresponding brain state. Brain states have been divided into roughly seven categories as follows:

Super High Beta	=	35 to 150 Hz
K-complex	=	33 to 35 Hz
High Beta	=	16 to 32 Hz
Beta	=	12 to 16 Hz
Theta	=	4 to 8 Hz
Delta	=	0.5 to 4 Hz

The least amount of energy in the brain occurs while the brain is in the Delta state. This state is sometimes called "the domain of sleep". There are no mental images and no awareness of the body. [1]

In the Theta state there can be visual images that seem very real, but little or no sense of the body is detected. Theta is the ideal state for some types of accelerated learning, self-programming and self-healing.

The Alpha state is the most well understood brain state. This is because, in this state, a person begins to become aware of his or her body and can supply biofeedback for purposes of studying this particular brain state. The body is very relaxed and training a subject to access the alpha state can greatly reduce stress and anxiety. Alpha has also been documented to accelerate learning by reducing the stress associated with learning.

Beta is associated with alertness and is our normal waking state. There is currently much research being done on the lower beta frequencies and their relation to learning. Drs. Joel and Judith Lubar from the University of Tennessee have discovered that persons with ADD are generally unable to generate Beta activity when trying to focus. In fact, when persons with ADD are trained to produce Beta activity, the ADD symptoms often decrease or disappear altogether. [2]

High Beta is the state of even greater alertness and seems to be related with states of anxiety or nervousness.

K-complex and Super-High Beta are just now being able to be explored with the advent of new technological devices. K-complex usually occurs in short bursts and scientists speculate that it is associated with periods of high creativity. Super-High Beta has had no controlled studies done upon it, but phenomena such as "out-of-body experiences" and powerful energy flows up the central nervous system have been associated with its activity. [3]

It is important to note that as brain wave activity slows down, changes also occur in respiration, muscle tension and awareness. IN FACT, ALL FOUR ELEMENTS SHARE A RECIPROCAL RELATIONSHIP. ALL OF THEM AFFECT EACH OTHER. So by changing the way we breathe, or relaxing certain muscles, or imagining specific situations, we can change our brain states and vice versa. Each has a dynamic influence on the way we learn and our ability to relax under test taking pressure. Let's study these influences individually.

PERFORMANCE BREATHING

The body can survive for weeks without food and days without drinking, but the brain can manage only 5 minutes without oxygen. One fourth of the oxygen in every breath is used to fuel the central nervous system. Breath control is a key component of emotional and performance control, but most people don't pay attention to their breathing and certainly are not taught how to use their breath for peak performance. As sure as a few minutes of panting or short, sporadic breathing can trigger a stress response, just as surely other breathing exercises can put you in control and into the peak performance state. [4]

The following breathing techniques are explained by Dr. James Loehr and Peter McLaughlin in their ground breaking book Mentally Tough and can be used to alter emotional states and brain states for optimal performance in the classroom, sports, and business.

The **Deep Abdominal Breath** is used for calming down and relaxing in a pressure situation and can be performed anywhere. Push your stomach out while taking in a deep breath through the nose and directing it into the abdomen for two counts followed by four counts of aiming the breath into the lungs. Exhale breathing out of the chest for a two count and then out of the abdomen for a six to eight count. Repeat the process for three or four breaths whenever you feel tense or nervous. This is a great breathing technique to use right before the test. [5]

The **Contrived Yawn** can be used when you feel bored or need to create interest in the task at hand. Your body will cause a yawn to occur periodically to enliven the nervous system, but you don't have to wait for a natural yawn to occur. Create a yawn by standing up. Then raise your hands over your head, push out your navel and take in all the air you can. Exhale vigorously and repeat three or four times. [6]

In order to face an immediate challenge successfully, there are two breathing techniques that provide instant oxygen and energy for optimal peak performance:

The **"HA" Breath** is simple. Tilt your head back and inhale deeply through your nose, then exhale forcefully through your mouth causing a loud "ha" sound. Repeat as needed. If you need to be more silent, use a quieter sound or simply force out the breath. This breath produces instant infusion of oxygen into the bloodstream providing more fuel to the brain and body. [7]

The **Energy Breath** the next breathing technique, works well when you feel sluggish and need some quick energy. Stand relaxed with arms at your side. On a slow steady inhalation, raise your arms outward until shoulder level, then move your arms in front of you and raise them over your head. Hold your breath a moment and then exhale out of your mouth as if blowing out a candle. While exhaling, drop your head, shoulders and neck. Repeat 5 to 10 times. [8]

Experiment with these breathing techniques to find which ones work for you. Research suggests that mental stress and anxiety can rob the brain of adequate oxygen by interrupting normal breathing patterns. This lack of oxygen results in disorientation, confusion, fatigue, and concentration and memory problems. The brain requires much more oxygen than any other organ of the body and even though it makes up only $1/50^{th}$ of the body's weight, it uses an amazing one-fifth of the body's oxygen supply. Use these techniques to keep the brain's oxygen flowing.

MUSCLE TENSION METHODS

Just as breathing influences muscle tension, awareness and brain states so does muscle tension influence breathing, brain states and awareness. By changing muscle tension or rearranging the way you move or hold your body, brain states can be altered almost immediately. There are extremely valuable techniques to be learned and applied when frustration or nervousness has forced us out of our peak performance state. Physical exercises like stretching or simply standing have been shown to adjust the chemical balance of the brain for increased stimulation by producing norepinephrine. This natural stimulation occurs without the nervousness or edginess associated with drugs and other stimulants. Here are some healthy suggestions on how to use the body to release nervous tension and produce a relaxed state.

Something as simple as standing has been shown to increase attention and learning power. Studies done at USC showed that standing increased heartbeats by 10 beats per minute, sending more blood to the brain and activating the central nervous system. Psychologically, standing up also creates more attention arousal allowing the brain to learn more. When energy seems to lag and focus is lost, **STAND UP!!**

A great way to release pent-up tension is to clench your fists as hard as you can while tensing up your arms and legs. Jerk your shoulders up as high as they will go and hold this uncomfortable position for 15 seconds. Close your eyes and imagine massive heavy leaden weights have been placed on top your shoulders. Release the weights by letting them slide down through your arms and legs as you slowly drop your shoulders. Repeat three times and the tension will leave your body, but energy and intensity will remain.

Another tension relieving exercise begins as you push your chair back from your desk and cross your arms around your chest. Begin to squeeze all the air out of your lungs. Squeeze real hard. As you push more air from your lungs, bend forward at the waist and squeeze to a count of eight. (See illustrations 1 & 2) Now relax your arms and upper body, inhale and gradually extend your arms up and out toward your head. Fill up your lungs as you reach as far up as you can. Repeat this cycle three times.

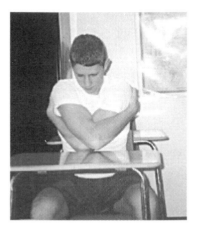

Illustration
1

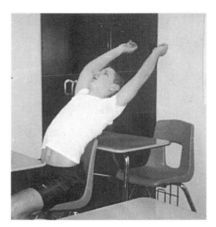

Illustration
2

A few minutes of vigorous exercise can help to clear your mind and lead to increased focus when you return to your task. Jumping rope with an imaginary rope would be good, or doing some walking around the room or on a treadmill is great for the brain. Quick calisthenics along with some stretching would be excellent for more energy and quick thinking.

Here are the most powerful techniques for using the body to achieve relaxation. The great news is that they can be used right before, and sometimes during, test taking sessions. They can also be utilized for peak performance in athletics and business.

Dr. Carla Hanniford, author of <u>Smart Moves,</u> describes a common stress problem as follows: "The 'tendon guard reflex' is an automatic process triggered by stress which shortens the calf muscle and locks the knees. The calf is the first muscle to tighten up when we become nervous or uptight and signals the lapse into **fight** or **flight** syndrome. When the back of the knees lock and the body moves forward onto the toes during stress, the rest of the body shifts to maintain balance. The muscles of the lower back and neck contract to keep us straight and balanced. This reflex is meant to occur only for a short time as we prepare to fight or run. But with such high levels of stress in our society today, many people end up with their knees, lower backs and necks almost perpetually locked". [9]

Some scientists believe that at the first sign of stress, if you stretch the calf muscle by doing what is called the calf pump (See Illustration A), you can avoid all the symptoms of fight or flight syndrome—sweaty palms, rapid heartbeat, shallow breathing and high blood pressure. The exercise can be done by holding the back of a chair and while keeping the torso upright, place one foot (with the heel up) about twelve inches behind the other foot. Take a deep breath and as you exhale, lower the heel of the back foot to the ground and bend the front knee forward. The calf pump is a great exercise to do before a test. If the test involves speaking or giving oral information, this exercise is extremely helpful because Dr. Hanniford has uncovered a peculiar link between the flexibility of the calf muscle and verbal skills. [10]

Another fantastic exercise for relaxation comes from Brain Gym exercises and is called The Hook Up. (See illustration B) Teachers and students can use this exercise when their stress levels rise and to refocus after interruptions. The exercise begins by first crossing one ankle over the other. Then stretch your arms out in front of you with the backs of the hands together and thumbs pointing down. Now lift one hand over the other, palms facing and intertwine the fingers. Then roll the locked hands straight down and in toward the body so they come to rest on the chest with the elbows down and shoulders relaxed. Now rest your tongue on the roof of your mouth just behind the front teeth (the hard palette). Notice the difference in muscle tightness and breathing and how the body is now handling the stress. [11]

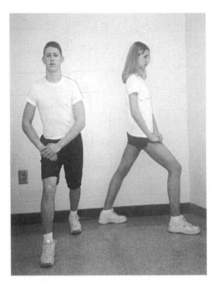

Illustration
A

Illustration
B

56

Another wonderful exercise combining brain hemisphere integration with relaxation is the Cross Crawl and it too comes from Brain Gym (See Illustration C). It is simply cross-lateral walking in place. Large areas of the brain are activated by touching right elbow to left knee and then left elbow to right knee. This exercise should be done very slowly with the student making sure to bring the elbows and knees across the center of the body. The cross-lateral movements facilitate faster and more integrated communication between the left and right brain hemispheres for high level reasoning and problem solving which result in stronger, more cohesive learning. These cross lateral movements have the effect of "waking up" the entire mind-body system while integrating both hemispheres of the brain. Use Cross Crawl when you feel stuck or in a slump, or for activating full mind-body function before mentally complicated or physically demanding activities. [12]

Experiment with these stretches and exercises or make up some of your own. Whatever works for you, continue to use it.

AWARENESS APPLICATIONS

The final method for changing brain states is to use your awareness or mental state. If you see a

gang of thugs approaching you, your awareness
causes you to have a completely different response

Illustration
C

than if you were sunning on a beach in Florida at
spring break. Visualization and fantasy can change
your brain states only because certain parts of the
brain cannot tell the difference between a real event
that is actually happening and an event that is viv-
idly imagined. Repetition is the key to mastering
this technique so that the brain becomes trained in
recognizing a new state.

Through the science of NeuroLinguistic Programming anyone can learn how to recreate or
switch brain states. All of our memories are made
up of what we saw, heard, felt, smelled, and tasted
at the time of the experience. Think back to your
high school prom and remember the song that was

playing while dancing the last dance. Or remember celebrating your 21st birthday, or playing in the championship game, or your wedding, or your first child being born. Each of these events creates specific feelings and memories that can change our brain state. These are called anchors because they "anchor" into our subconscious the feelings, smells, sights and sounds of our memories and allow us to recreate them whenever we wish. Have you ever walked into a room and a particular melody was playing and this melody brought back memories and feelings of events that had occurred when you heard this song being played at an emotional or important event in your life? The song became part of the memory. This **"anchoring"** technique is used by salespeople and professional athletes to recreate the feelings, emotions and sensations of an upset victory or a big sale because creating the memory may also recreate the performance!

When someone tells you to "go to your happy place" to change your attitude, they are actually giving you great advice. Most of us would tend to shrug this advice off, but it is possible to create our own anchor for the purposes of motivation, relaxation, and learning.

One of the best descriptions of creating an anchor comes from Tom Kenyon, M.A., in his book Brain States as follows:

1. Sit comfortably and close your eyes.
2. Recall a pleasant experience, something that gives you pleasure to think about.
3. Now focus on the *feeling* of pleasure and not the experience itself.
4. Make this feeling of pleasure as strong as you can.
5. As you recreate this strong and pleasant feeling, let your body get into a position where the feeling is the strongest. For instance, if you felt proud, sit or stand upright. If you were sad, slump over. Let your body be in the position that feels natural to you for this feeling. As you feel the feeling and hold your body in this position, touch your thumb and first finger together, or reach down and touch your thigh. Sense this gesture at the same time you feel the intensified pleasant feeling. Hold the touch, body position, and the feeling together for a few moments.
6. Release the touch and the feeling. Bring yourself back to neutral with no particular feeling.
7. Without changing your feeling, touch yourself in the exact same way, and at the exact same location, as you move your body in the position you took in step #5.
8. Notice that as you hold this touch and this position, the feeling tends to come back.
9. Go through this exercise again and again

until you feel these two anchors (your touch and body position) stimulating and recreating that pleasant feeling. Sometimes the anchors take hold after the first try, sometimes several trys are required. Do not be impatient with yourself—mastery comes from repetition. Stick with it and it will happen. [13]

After reading this chapter, you will know more about relaxation and how to access the peak performance state than most people in our country. Use this information to increase test scores, make more sales or score more goals.

The power is yours—USE IT!!

CHAPTER 4

I is for
INDIVIDUALITY

$\mathcal{P}$robably the neatest thing about being human is that every one of us is different. That's what makes us beautiful and unique. We look different, we feel differently, we react differently **AND WE ALL LEARN DIFFERENTLY!**

It will become a distinct advantage in learning, memory, and test taking if, by self-discovery, you can determine the way that your brain and body learn the best. This bit of knowledge can make learning fun and test taking a breeze. It is well worth the time to find out about learning styles and intelligences. Use this information to develop specific, personal strategies for power learning and testing.

Some of the pioneers in the field of intelligence are Robert Sternberg, Stephan Ceci, and David Feldman, but Howard Gardner and his colleagues developed the theory of multiple intelligences. The theory states that every individual possesses several different and independent capacities for solving problems and learning.

The good news is there are 8 intelligences at your disposal that you can use for optimum learning and performance. You'll also be happy to know that you were born with all eight of these intelligences! However, certain influences in your life and in your environment have caused some intelligences to develop more strongly than others and some not to develop at all. More good news is that each intelligence can be taught, nurtured, modified and expanded for full development. Each of us has tremendous power over personal learning and memory if we can determine the primary styles and intelligences used for the actual learning. The more intelligences and styles you can bring into the learning, the stronger the learning will become and the easier it will be to recall the learning and use it on an everyday basis.

The following are short discussions of each of the 8 intelligences including descriptions of the intelligence, how we can tell if the intelligence fits us, and what can be done to increase the effectiveness of the intelligence.

The first intelligence is **Verbal/Linguistic Intelligence**. It is the talent to use our language. People of this intelligence use words while they are thinking and they express themselves very clearly. They enjoy reading, writing, listening and speaking. They respond well to encouragement, but are hindered tremendously by criticism, negative comments and humiliation. Learning is enhanced for this student by using cooperative learning techniques, peer teaching, dramatic readings and guest speakers. [1]

Musical/Rhythmic is another intelligence. It is the ability to use the musical elements of pitch, rhythm, tone and sound. This learner loves to hear the sounds around them and to respond to them with action (toe-tapping, head-tilting). They love melody and keeping a beat. Soft background music can help this student focus, but random noise and harsh sounds distract them. This student needs to move and not sit for long periods of time doing repetitive tasks. For this student, learning can be enhanced by allowing them to create jingles, raps, cheers and songs that pertain to the learning. [2]

Logical/Mathematical is the next intelligence. It is the ability to use inductive and deductive reasoning, solve abstract problems, and understand complex relationships. This learner loves calculations, problem solving, interpreting data and using technology. He or she also relies heavily upon the tools of the trade like calculators and computers. This intelligence likes everything in order and thrives on organization and enjoys making predictions based on facts, but finds it difficult to work in chaos and confusion. When rushed and without an opportunity to reason or interpret, this learner will shut down. Puzzles, games, experiments, research, analogies and mnemonics will help promote learning in this intelligence. [3]

Visual/Spacial Intelligence is the capacity to perceive or "see" the world accurately and to recreate visual experiences. It uses the ability to see form, color, shape and texture. These learners are creative and inventive using color and pictures to form patterns and impressions. This learner loves color in the environment and uses collages, illustrations and filmstrips to enhance learning, but is turned off by dull, colorless environments and assignments that force the use of words and description. Cameras, posters, charts, pretending, and graphic rich environments aid this intelligence. [4]

Bodily/Kinesthetic Intelligence establishes the mind-body connection and allows for control of the body and interpretation of body movements. In other words, physical talent. These learners enjoy sports and movement and are equipped with good timing and sense of direction. These learners need to be able to move and stretch and display emotions and are hindered by invasion of their space, dead time, long lectures and isolation. Techniques to aid learning include field trips, role playing, stretching breaks, simulations and any type of active learning. [5]

The Naturalist has the ability to use nature to survive and adapt. These learners are concerned about the environment and curious about all of nature. They enjoy using their curiosity and intuition and they do very well in science. They also like to take chances and enjoy taking risks. Let them sit by the window or go outdoors for class on nice days. These students must feel accepted or they could shut down. Nature collections, survival exercises, use of natural resources, wellness and fitness, and nature walks are ways to reach this learner. [6]

Intrapersonal Intelligence is the ability to know one's self and to use this information for success in life. This learner likes to daydream and reflect. They are confident and very determined. They possess tremendous insight and powerful interpretation skills. This student does well when given choices in the learning process. They perform well when left alone, but find it hard to adhere to schedules. And they dislike harsh punishments. This learner needs to be given a reason why something is being done. These students are very uncomfortable with standardized tests. Activities to promote learning for this intelligence include goal-setting, journals, visualization, silent reflection time, imagery and self-discovery. [7]

Interpersonal Intelligence is social talent. Simply put, these learners understand, get along with, and motivate others. They like to study people and cultures as well as history and art. They like organized instruction for groups or pairs and they thrive when involved in entire-class activities. But these students hate working alone and learn very little without outside personal influences. Creative, cooperative tasks using group activities are best for this learner. [8]

Now that you may have discovered your primary intelligence, you can begin to develop learning, studying and test taking habits that will increase the amount of learning you will be able to use and remember. The habits that work best for you will depend on your individual learning style.

In study after study researchers have verified that learning can require many different approaches and that learners perform best in their own learning style. The research also proves that when learners are taught in their individual style, their motivation, initiative, and results improve dramatically. Even apathetic learners become enthusiastic when learning is offered in their preferred style.

If you want to determine your individual learning style, ask your teacher or guidance counselor for a <u>Dunn, Dunn and Price Learning Styles Inventory</u> assessment. There is also a version to be used in the home called "Amazing Grades" by Dr. Kenneth Dunn and can be ordered at Unlimited Learning, Inc. at 12377 Merit Drive, Suite 1140 LB 90, Dallas, TX 75251 or by calling 214-387-8077.

There are 22 important elements of learning styles that can be grouped into five categories: environmental, emotional, learning groups, sensory and biological. The following paragraphs provide an overview of each of these categories. HINT: As you read through the list, notice whether you have a strong reaction to any of these styles or characteristics. Then do some experimenting with those specific elements to see if your studying or test taking becomes more productive.

ENVIRONMENTAL

1. **Noise level**—do you need quiet or sound. Some learners need sound while others are distracted by it. Other students can block out sound while still others need noise and activity around them as they study.
2. **Light**—Some students like bright light, others find it harsh and irritating and need dim light to concentrate.
3. **Temperature**—Many students think best when it's hot, others when they feel cold.
4. **Setting**—is the preference for informal or formal? Would the learner prefer plastic or steel chairs compared to beds, the floor, or bean bag chairs. What else could be done

to improve the environment for individual style? Perhaps an aquarium or a few houseplants or possibly a new coat of paint. Use your individual learning style and imagination to experiment with your personal learning environment. [9]

EMOTIONS AND ATTITUDES

5. **Motivation**—Some people desire to achieve in school and others care about different areas of their lives.
6. **Persistence**—Do you tackle a task head on and stay with it until completion? Or do you prefer to take breaks and gradually see projects through to the end? How do you feel about time limits and deadlines?
7. **Responsibility**—Do you follow through and do what is asked of you? Or do you need to be more involved in the decision making and planning of a project?
8. **Structure**—Do you need instructions and explanations or do you enjoy completing assignments your own way in your own time? [10]

LEARNING GROUPS

9. **Learning alone**—these learners prefer to

study by themselves.

10. **Pairs**—these students like to work with one other person.

11. **Teams**—these pupils enjoy group learning with lots of discussion and interaction.

12. **Authority Figure Present**—these learners prefer that someone with authority or special knowledge is present while the studying or learning is taking place.

13. **Prefers Variety**—these learners can use any one of the group styles or would prefer a variety of offerings instead of the same ones every time. [11]

SENSORY

14. **Auditory**—best learning occurs while listening.

15. **Visual Words**—learns primarily by seeing and reading words.

16. **Visual Pictures**—this learner can easily recall what is seen and is adept at creating pictures out of words.

17. **Tactual or Touching**—this student needs to examine the object of his learning "hands on". Keep those hands busy while learning.

18. **Kinesthetic or Doing/Moving**—this

student requires whole body movement for optimal learning. He or she absorbs learning best through real life experiences. This learning is enhanced further when the student is totally involved in the experience. [12]

BIOLOGICAL

19. Requires Intake—some students often eat, drink, chew or bite while concentrating as opposed to other students that require no intake until after the task is finished.

20. Time of Day—any learner would benefit from researching their daily rhythms and discovering the best times of day for learning new or difficult material.

21. Mobility—Some pupils need to sit quietly while learning while others need to take frequent breaks and be constantly moving.

22. Global/Analytic—Some learners like to see the whole picture first and to know what the final goal will be. Others like to start at the beginning and proceed step by step using trial and error. They enjoy learning as they go along and revel in the slightest of discoveries. [13]

While you were reading these descriptions, did you learn anything about the way you like to learn? Sometimes at school we just can't seem to understand the material, but at home, working alone, we can learn it in half the time. This could be directly related to your learning style. Most students will instinctually use the methods and techniques that work for their style without even being aware of it. But wouldn't it make sense to begin adapting strategies that would utilize our learning style to the fullest extent? Self-discovery can make learning fun and effortless. It only takes one small discovery to product fantastic results.

For instance, if you are an **Auditory**, concentrate very hard on what's being said in class and use a tape recorder, if allowed, to tape the lesson. When taking tests, read the directions out loud back to yourself for best understanding. Add an accent to your voice while reading material and use various voice inflections to further cement the learning into your memory.

Another example would be that after you discover your **body/brain** cycle or rhythm, you can alter your schedule to study for the test or learn new material *at the specific time of day when your brain is working at full capacity*! You can find out all you need to know about your brain, body, and learning styles simply by experimenting.

If you have strengths in **Visual-Word**, you might want to try reading assignments related to the lecture the night before or the day before the lecture is to be given. The specific time you read this material would depend upon your "time of day" style.

If you are a **Kinesthetic** learner, try walking or moving your body while learning new material. Use stretching and breathing exercises before and during study periods. Experiment with different positions (reclining versus standing or sitting versus lying down) and types of seating (hard wooden seats versus bean bag chairs).

Continue to always be curious about yourself and creative about experimenting with your individual style. The knowledge you discover could hold the keys to your personal success.

While doing my research, I learned some specific techniques about different learning styles that can increase the effectiveness of test taking skills and study habits. These discoveries come from research done within the science of NeuroLinguistic Programming (NLP) and are explained below.

You can determine a person's *sensory* learning style by listening to the verbs and descriptive words they use during conversation. If they keep saying "I see what you mean" or "I can picture that", then they are probably visual learners. If someone uses phrases like "that rings a bell" or "I hear what you're saying", then they are probably auditory learners.

Using NLP, you can tell a person's learning style by becoming aware of their eye movements! Ask someone a question about the past or future and observe their eyes. One of the following might occur.

Visual learners will look up before answering questions about the past or future, usually glancing to the left if the question is about the past or glancing to the right if the question requires them to think or visualize the future. Neuroscientists explain this phenomena because looking up activates the visual cortex of the brain, giving the visual learner a useful tool to help them change their visions into words and allowing them to answer the question.

** This bit of information can come in very handy during a learning or testing situation. When learning new material, the learner (especially visuals) should sit below the teacher so that they have to look up when digesting the learning. The brain will be able to process more information. Also, if you use motivational signs or posters in the classroom or locker room, make sure they are above eye level so the reader has to look up to read them. This will help lock the messages in the subconscious mind.

** If a learner is having trouble spelling have them try this technique. If the word comes from the past and they have already been taught the word, encourage them to look up and to the left while visualizing the word. If the word is from the future or if the word is new to the learner (possibly the student is spelling it for the first time or creating a new word), instruct him or her to look up and to the right while visualizing the word. Some studies actually show a 5 to 12% increase in the ability to spell correctly using this method! Using a standard grading scale, that can mean the difference between a "B" or "C" simply by using one new technique!

NLP information about eye movement is also used by the CIA when they don't have access to a lie detector and by police stations when questioning suspects to determine if they are lying. When a person is asked a question about past or future and they look up and to the right before they answer, then there is a powerful chance they are lying. Why? Because he or she is accessing the creative part of the brain and thinking in the future, constructing visions that have not yet happened. In other words, the person is making it up or creating the answer—*THEY ARE LYING TO YOU!* If looking to the left, they are reconstructing events from the past that have already happened and chances are, they are probably telling the truth. Did you ever wonder why, when the best poker players in the world get together to play the "World Series of Poker" in Las Vegas, they are all wearing sunglasses? Why would they need sunglasses in those dimly lit, smoke-filled rooms? Or why do certain negotiators wear dark glasses when working out business deals or settling international relations? The reason is because these poker players and deal-makers certainly don't want the other side knowing when they are lying or bluffing. The eyes can truly be the windows to the soul! [14]

Auditory learners look straight ahead and to the left (past) or right (future) when answering questions. Approximately 25% of our population are auditory learners. One characteristic of auditory learners is that they sometimes mumble and talk to themselves. Use this information by talking to yourself out loud when reading directions or working out problems. Talking to yourself can be even more effective if you use different pitches and paces in your speech. The changing of the voice inflection has been shown to activate more areas of the brain while listening!

Kinesthetic learners use their feelings and body

for learning. A person's eye movement when they are experiencing emotion will usually be down and to the right. Therefore, when asked a question about the past or future, a kinesthetic learner will look down and to the right. This allows them to put their feelings and emotions into words and answer the question. Kinesthetic learners will sometimes appear to be slow thinkers, but that is only because it takes a few moments longer to access feelings and emotions than it does for a visual to create a picture or an auditory to process a sound.

   **Kinesthetic learners need to sit comfortably while taking tests. They also need more time to process their feelings into answers. They should also experiment to discover at what temperature they perform the best. When taking tests in uncomfortable chairs or if the temperature in the room is too hot or too cold, some kinesthetic learners will be unable to access information or to think clearly.

   Another tip for kinesthetic learners (which is about 40% of the population) is to use the body and its motions to help them anchor in learning. The hand and mouth hold the most nerve receptors than in any other parts of the body. This is why kinesthetic learners will sometimes connect their hands to their mouths when answering questions........ (See Illustration 3). If someone you know continually takes on the posture in (Illustration 3), it is almost dead certain that he or she is primarily a kinesthetic learner. Certain studies conducted which allowed kinesthetic students to squeeze stress balls, *while learning new material* indicated that learning capacity was increased while using motion during the learning.

Illustration
3

As you can see, learning about yourself can provide you with very powerful information. Discovering your personal style while learning about your specific intelligences can enhance your test taking ability almost immediately. These same techniques can also be used to guarantee your success in life. Successful life is continual learning. Never stop learning about yourself and the world around you. Always be curious! Experiment all the time! Use your discoveries to grow a little bit every day and experience the joys of constant learning and continuous improvement in whatever you do. **GO FOR IT!!!**

CHAPTER 5

V is for VISUALIZING CONFIDENCE

*I*n my opinion, this is the most important chapter in this book. The most crucial element in life upon which everything depends is **BELIEF!** BELIEF is what determines success or failure in whatever we do. Whether the goal is achieving higher test scores, making the big sale, or scoring the game-winning goal, BELIEF determines what the final outcome will be! BELIEF goes by many names—confidence, self-assuredness, self-esteem, or positive attitude. But no matter what you call it, it is the greatest gift we can give to our children.

Everything that happens in our children's lives—what career they choose, how much money they make, who they will marry, where they will live, what position they hold in the company—all goes back to **BELIEF**. Will they participate in sports, try out for the school drama production, or learn to play a musical instrument? Will they own their own company or become CEO in someone else's? Will they have the courage to pursue dreams? Confidence is the key to answering these questions. Winners take more risks than losers do and belief in oneself is what gives winners the confidence to take more risks and chances. If students believe they can learn, they will! If students believe that they are good test takers, their grades will soar!

In this chapter you can learn how to give the

gift of confidence and self-belief to yourself, your children and all those around you.

Let's go for it!

Countless studies by Robert Rosenthal, L. Jacobson, James Beatty, Stephanie Madon, Kathryn Kolb, and others suggest that when positive attitude is activated and high expectations are set at the beginning of class, then learning success increases. Always set high expectations and verbalize confidence in the ability to achieve these expectations. Scientists have shown that strong confident attitudes allow the body to relax and produce neurotransmitters like dopamine and noradrenaline increasing alertness and energy. This in turn activates the frontal lobes regulating judgement, planning, and concentration skills. Be aware of the self-fulfilling prophecy where negative expectations produce negative results and positive expectations yield positive results. When test takers anticipate positive results their test scores rise!

Jane Richards and James Gross conducted a study in the year 2000 for *The Journal of Personality & Social Psychology* and published their findings in the September issue. Their research concluded that an optimistic attitude improves memory under stressful conditions. Developing a positive attitude lessened the need for second guessing and self-monitoring, freeing up the brain to better learn and remember new information. It is important to teach learners techniques for handling stress (deep breathing, music therapy, stretching) and to incorporate self-esteem building methods into their education.

How can we build this type of belief into our test takers? Here are some of the most powerful techniques available for changing attitudes and belief. When deciding which of these methods you would like to implement first, be sure to read Chapter 4 and discover what style and intelligence work the best for the learner. For optimum success, chose the techniques that employ the most elements of the individual learning style. If not possible, alter the technique so that it will fit or work with a specific style. Throughout this chapter, suggestions will be given on how to apply these techniques to the various learning styles and intelligences.

VISUALIZATION

Many researchers have called Visualization the most important tool possessed by the human mind for goal achievement and success in school, sports and business. And yet, this powerful tool is not taught in the schools. We leave the visualization process to be figured out by the students themselves through trial and error, experimentation, extra study or special seminars. Some students never learn how to increase the intensity or control the tremendous power of their visions and dreams. This is truly sad since every great achievement in the history of mankind was begun with a dream or vision. If you can see it, you can achieve it!

Practice the following NeuroLinguistic Programming skills. They are fun and easy to use and will help to make your visualizations extremely powerful. Some of these exercises may seem easier to perform than others. This is because each learner is more adept at certain modalities than they are at others. The key here is to experiment with individual feelings, visions, and sounds to find the correct combination for you.

First of all, we know that looking up activates the visual cortex. Therefore, this next eye exercise will be great for "warming up" the brain before any visualization and putting the brain in the correct state to "see" the visualizations more clearly and completely. (Illustration D) While keeping your nose pointed straight ahead, look up with both eyes and move them sideways, back and forth like you were scanning the sky above you. Go back and forth at least 5 times to activate the visual cortex. Now you are ready.

Illustration
D

When visualizing, you may be more comfortable with your eyes closed. Or maybe with your
eyes open. This will depend on your individual
intelligence discussed in Chapter 4. If you are an
auditory, it may help to have some classical, soft
jazz, or new wave music playing in the background.
Notice all the ingredients that make the vision
"better" for you and use those particular elements
or modalities.

If you a kinesthetic learner, it will help to associate a feeling or emotion with the vision and recreate this feeling in your body. To see yourself as a
confident test taker, incorporate relaxing breathing
patterns into your vision. Learn to "feel" the power
of your knowledge and ability. Push your chest out
and pull the shoulders back. Picture yourself sitting
up straight, eager to take the test with a confident

smile on your face. Possibly add powerful music like the theme from Rocky or Superman. Speed the music up at times and then slow it down. "Hear" which one works the best. Use different music for different visualizations. Some athletes and students have actually been able to anchor their visualizations to certain pieces of music. Use your humor and talent to experiment and create personal, powerful visualizations.

Experiment with the images by adding or subtracting different qualities and properties. What emotions do you feel if you see the images in color or black and white? Which one "feels" better to you? Put a frame around the picture and then take it away. Which is better? See the images as flowing and rhythmic and then make them perfectly still. Which do you prefer? See the images up close and then far away, see them clear and sharp, then fuzzy and unfocused. Notice your emotional reaction to all these changes and take notes in your journal. Stick with the properties that make you "feel" and "see" the best.

To make our visions more powerful, learn to associate emotions with the images. The more intense the emotion, the deeper the learning is embedded. While visualizing, notice where on your body you are feeling your emotion. When you are sad, what does your face look like? Are you slumped over? What's your breathing like? Learn about yourself and discover what is best for you.

While visualizing, train your mind to always see positive performance. If you have trouble seeing what you desire to happen then SLOW THE IMAGES DOWN. Your mind can be used as a VCR. Slow the vision down so much that you can't help but succeed. Rewind the picture over and over until you get it right. Never let yourself imagine a failure—rewind the image and erase it and then see it happening successfully.

Another fun activity that can help you visualize is to construct a collage with the central theme being how you want to look and feel while taking a test. Collect magazine photos and newspaper headlines and intersperse actual photos of yourself studying, working hard (but having fun), and cel-ebrating your great grades and accomplishments. Look at this collage before you take the test or hang it in your locker or post it on your bedroom ceiling. Be creative.

Earlier in this book, you learned how to create an anchor. Visualization is another tool to use when forming an anchor. The following is an ex-cerpt from my tape program "Turning Slumps Into Streaks" that explains how to form an anchor using visualization.This excerp contains some additional tips on how to make your visualization more powerful:

"Here is an extremely powerful tool that you can use to feel positive and perform at a peak level any time you desire. It's called anchoring. The best way to explain it is to ask you if you have ever been driving on a highway and your favorite song came on the radio. What happened? Did you smile, start tapping your feet, maybe some chair dancing? But you felt great, didn't you? That is an anchor. Or maybe Mom was cooking your favorite meal and you smelled it as you walked in the door. Did your mouth water? Did you put your nose in the air and try to take in as much of the aroma as you could or did you just feel like hugging mom. That is also an anchor.

Using all you have learned so far, here is how you can establish an anchor to enhance your performance. Start by finding <u>your</u> most comfortable position in <u>your</u> most comfortable chair. Put on some Mozart or calm, relaxing music. Now begin to visualize using all the preferences you've established from your personal learning style and intelligence. Picture a moment in time when everything was going your way. You were "in the zone". This can be a moment from school, sports, or personal life. What did the experience smell like? How did it feel? Were you sweating, was it hot or cool, was it raining? RELIVE the moment—hear the crowd, feel the excitement, see the results. After a time, you will actually get a chill down your spine or maybe your neck will tingle or you'll get goosebumps. *THAT'S THE MOMENT, ANCHOR IT!!* You can anchor it by simply tugging your ear lobe, slapping your thigh or clenching your fist. But use something physical and personal. It's your anchor, you decide.

Do this every day. It may take a while at first, but in time (usually 2 to 3 weeks, but in some individuals, ONCE) all you will have to do is tug your ear or slap your thigh and the feelings of greatness will be there. This feeling is a tremendous difference when compared to the feelings of distress and discomfort associated with a pressure situation."

You may want to use your anchor as part of your pre-test ritual. Now you are probably wondering what a ritual is. A ritual is a mental cue used by all peak performers to build confidence, relax, get in the right moment, avoid distractions, feel power-

ful, and much more. **WOW!!** Sounds like powerful stuff—and it is! Do you have a ritual? If not,
you'd better get one.

Watch the best foul shooters, field goal kickers,
sales people, managers, hitters in baseball and
softball, and almost anyone that excels at what they
do—they all use rituals. Ivan Lendl would bounce
the ball the same number of times whenever he
served, Bill Russell would throw up before the
game (Ugh), Mary Lou Retton would visualize
before each event, and Jeff Hornacek or the Utah
Jazz rubs his cheek three times before each foul
shot (for him this is both a ritual and an anchor
because that gesture is also a code between him and
his children watching the game at home—neat,
huh?). Luciano Pavarotti finds a restaurant in the
city where he is performing and cooks dinner for
the patrons. He then goes to the opera house early
to put on costume and makeup so that he can enter-
tain the rest of the cast while they are readying for
the performance. Erric Pegram of the Pittsburgh
Steelers watched episodes of *Sanford and Son* to
loosen up for the big game. The list goes on and
on.

Most professionals use rituals to avoid distractions and to start their performance with something
that feels comfortable. Others believe it helps them
get in the groove and to relax. All the above are
true.

Now that you see how important rituals are to performance, ask yourself what your rituals are. If you don't have any then make some and **DO IT NOW!**

After reading this far, you have all kinds of ammunition and knowledge to develop your personal "power rituals". For instance, you could use a special breathing ritual before the test to supply more oxygen to the brain and relax the body. Or possibly an eating ritual using the correct types and varieties of foods to produce mental alertness. Or even a stretching ritual loosening all the muscles to allow for relaxation and super memory and thinking skills. Or maybe something as simple as wearing your lucky socks! Use your anchor as a ritual or your visualization experience—the possibilities are limitless.

A fantastic ritual would be to have your very own personal pep assembly. It's true. Did you ever walk into a test thinking "I'm terrible at Math" or "I'm not a good test taker" or "I'm going to flunk"—well, you need a PEP RALLY! The above examples are called "self-talk" and the things we say to ourselves before a test can actually "set-up" or determine how we will really perform. This is called a self-fulfilling prophecy. Most students fill themselves with self-doubt and have failed before they even attempt the exam. This needs to be changed if that student will ever experience success.

The best way to change self-talk and to build confidence instead of tearing it down is called AFFIRMATION TRAINING. Simply put, affirmations are saying positive things to ourselves about ourselves. It could be considered a form of self advertising. Muhammed Ali did it everyday when he said "I am the greatest". He said it over and over to anyone that would listen until, finally, he actually became the greatest.

Affirmations have to be used in a very specific way to be effective. First, determine the exact way you would like to perform or choose a personality trait or characteristic you would like to possess. It is important that the affirmation you create be in the first person, using present tense like it is already happening in your life. Here are some examples:

> I am always calm and confident under
>   pressure.
> I am a super test taker.
> I solve problems very quickly under
>   pressure.
> I am a fast thinker.

Avoid negative terms and always make your affirmations positive. Using words like hate (I hate my job), can't (I can't do this), or never (I'll never set the record) limit your ability and lead to inflexible thinking. Think of the many things you say to yourself on a daily basis that put limits on your life. Using negative contractions like can't, won't, or couldn't are especially limiting because of the effect they have on the brain. The brain thinks in pictures, but has great difficulty with negative contractions because it can't associate a picture to them. You can't see a "won't" and you can't touch a "wouldn't"—therefore, your brain acts like the negative contraction isn't there and only hears what follows. For instance, if I tell you "don't think of Tom Cruise", what are you thinking about? The same thing happens when you tell yourself "don't choke on this test" or "don't be nervous". Your brain only hears "choke on this test" and "be nervous" and the brain always does what it is told. Instead tell yourself you are calm and confident or that you can relax easily and the results will come.

Research indicates that the best way to say an affirmation is to repeat each of them three times using different voice inflections and body movements with each repetition. This helps all the areas of the brain absorb the good news about yourself.

A powerful time to use your affirmations is in the morning upon awakening because they start your day positively and will stay with you all day long. Did you ever set your alarm to your favorite radio station and a song was playing when you woke up? Did you find that same song going over and over in your head all morning? The same will happen with your affirmations and you'll be reminded of your power all day long.

Another great time to practice your positive statements is in the evening before bed. Research indicates that your subconscious mind will help you work on your affirmations all night long while sleeping if they are recited as you are going to bed.

Also, repeat your affirmations just before the test. They will activate the brain for peak performance and build confidence while allowing you to relax and believe in yourself.

Remember that thoughts repeated become believed and thoughts believed become reality. If you don't believe that you can actually change the way you think and feel by repeating things over and over, then take this test. Have you ever been to Disney World? I'll bet you went on a ride with your family called "It's a Small World".
Well, when you got off that ride, what song were you humming to yourself for the next few hours?
THAT'S HOW AFFIRMATIONS WORK. If you repeat them enough, they'll come into your mind when you need them the most. But as with any-

thing else, **IT TAKES PRACTICE.**

When you were very young (think back now), you were persistent and tried everything. You were also a fantastic learner. In fact, most people learn more in their first five years than they do for all the rest of their life! This is mainly due to the positive feedback that most babies get. When you were learning to walk and you fell down, did people tell you things like "Forget it, stupid, you'll never be able to do that" or "stop that, you'll get hurt"? No, they didn't. They encouraged you and made you feel great and told you to keep trying.

Then, at various times in our life, the negative programming started. Parents will sometimes tell their kids that they can't do things simply because they weren't able to do them. They also don't want their children to be hurt physically or emotionally by the experience of failure. Studies indicate that by the time the average student is 18, they have already heard over 200,000 times—"no", "don't", or "you can't do that". By the time a child is 6 years old, they have already seen on television, 47,000 random acts of violence. During the early years, a child can generally block out these negative phrases and experiences for about two to four years, but then the child begins to believe their limitations and the failure programming begins to stick and take its toll. It can sometimes be very difficult to overcome this negativity, but here are some techniques that will help.

Kimberly Kassner in her book <u>EmpowerMind for Teens</u> describes a very powerful technique called the Treasure Chest. To use this method, students make a personal file containing all the wonderful things they've accomplished in their lives. Souvenirs from these moments and experiences are collected and kept in a Treasure Chest. Some items might be the newspaper article about making the game-winning basket, the program from the school play or choral recital, photographs taken at school and athletic events. Other materials might include a personal scrapbook, and a success journal filled with feelings experienced during these precious moments. Included would be momentos from your friends, thank-you cards, invitations, ribbons for achievement, trophies, poems, love letters, "A" papers, and anything that makes you feel good about yourself and realize the many amazing things you are capable of achieving in your life. Go to your treasure chest when feeling down about your abilities or just because you are having a bad day and it will turn your attitude and your mood completely around. [1]

To help you remember about your greatness, keep a success journal. Write down all the fantastic things you've already accomplished in life and update the list daily or weekly. If you don't write things down, you will forget them. Keep reviewing the list periodically for added personal power.

Another way to help you continually upgrade your journal and build esteem in children is a technique that I heard Oprah Winfrey discuss on her TV show. It was revealed that Oprah has used this specific technique since childhood and credits it with her success. Each night before bed make it a practice to list 5 things in your life that you were thankful for that day. It's a very simple task but can add power to your life. If you want to see real power adapt this practice to include the whole family. Have everyone share at least 3 things that they did that day that made a difference in someone's life. Also, have each person mention a problem they are having and ask for solutions— you'll be surprised at how quickly people start feeling great about themselves and how problems start to disappear. In our hectic world this is also an awesome way to stay in touch with each other and find out exactly what is happening in each other's lives.

You can also add a very effective technique suggested by Earl Nightengale. Earl used to call compliments "golden bricks" and he suggested making it a point to each day throw at least 3 "golden bricks" at someone. In other words, give them a compliment or notice them doing something right and tell them about it. It won't take long for attitude and environment to elevate to new heights.

Many times students have difficulty seeing themselves as being successful or recognizing the traits they already possess to achieve success. To help recognize these traits while building confidence, try this method. List your three most powerful strengths and then your three most glaring weaknesses on a sheet of paper. Then ask some classmates, your parents, some coaches, your siblings and your parents to make their suggestions about what they feel are your strengths and weaknesses. You will find that each person, including yourself, has a different opinion of you, your strengths and your weaknesses, but there will also be some similarities. Write down all the positive comments on a sheet of paper. Then write down all the negative comments on another sheet of paper.

Now comes the important part. We are going to make a **PLAN**. For every positive comment, write down at least two action steps that you could perform that would make each strength you possess even stronger. For the negative comments, write down at least two action steps that could be taken immediately to eliminate the weaknesses. Concentrate on how you can maintain or increase your strengths while at the same time improving your weaknesses. If you have trouble coming up with ideas on how to improve, ask your sources. I know they'll be happy to help and it will strengthen your relationships. Then make a deal with yourself to work on at least one item from each list every day for the next month. After the month is over, evaluate where you are now compared to where you were before. You will find the results amazing! **Start this TODAY!**

Another technique for developing confidence and discovering a roadmap to success is called mentoring or modeling. This procedure makes a lot of sense and is relatively easy to begin. First, find someone who has already achieved the success you desire. Find out who always manages to have great test scores and high grades and then arrange an interview with them, read about them, ask their friends about them or simply start hanging out with them. Discover the habits and patterns you need to acquire or develop in order to become a super student and then DO WHAT YOU NEED TO DO! Start modeling their behavior and an amazing thing occurs—you start getting better grades and higher test scores!! Find a student that is always on the Honor Roll or Dean's List and mimic their behavior and you can be on the Honor Roll too. Think about it, most of us already know how to be "C" students and we keep modeling that behavior and remain "C" students. Who could you seek out and talk to today that would be able to improve your grades and raise your test scores? *CALL THEM NOW!*

The most powerful tool for success that is used by ONLY 3% of our population is Goal Setting. Goal Setting is a mandatory, essential, and fool-proof way to achieve anything you desire in life, and yet again, this powerful skill is not taught in most school systems!

When is the last time you set a goal? If you are like most people, you have never set one! I believe we have heard so much about goal setting from so many different people that we take goals for granted and simply don't set them. There are no classes in school for this life-altering skill and the only way we learn how to set goals is to go to a seminar specifically about goal setting or associate with people that have achieved great success through goal setting. If you are afraid to set goals because of the pressure they will put on you to succeed, then try setting mini-goals on 3x5 note cards. This is a great way to start and will teach you the skills you need to tackle those big goals.

Remember, we are starting simple. So TODAY write a goal down on a 3x5 notecard. Make it something you know you can accomplish in one day's time with little effort. Write it down using positive words and give yourself a deadline of this evening. Then write down three things (it might be less if your goal is simple) you must do today to achieve your goal. Sit for a few seconds and visualize yourself achieving your goal. Use all your senses as you see your success. See it in color, smell it, taste it, feel how good it is going to be when you accomplish your goal. Put the goal in your pants pocket or in your purse where you keep your change and keys, or tape it to a notebook you tend to use often throughout the day. Even better, make copies and put them everywhere. The object is to continually remind yourself all day long about your goal.

This next step is very important. Never leave the scene where you set your goal without doing the first step to achieve it. In other words, do the first action step RIGHT NOW! Look at your goal card numerous times throughout the day and plan the time to do your action steps.

Tonight, after your goal is achieved, do something nice for yourself. See a movie, buy an ice cream cone or simply watch your favorite television program. How does that feel?

The last step is to do it all over again tomorrow and then the next day, aiming a little higher each day. Pretty soon your goals will be so big you'll need a week, month and then a year to accomplish them. The only thing that will be different is that now you know that eventually, they will become reality.

HINT: Always put your goals down on paper. Goals kept in the head usually go unfulfilled. A dull pencil is better than the sharpest mind!

Here's proof: A Harvard Business School study found that 83% of our population have no clearly defined goals, mental or written. It also found that 14% have goals, but the goals are not written down. Only 3% of the population actually have goals that are written down. So just by writing down a goal, you are in the top 3% of the population—Congratulations!! But here's the kicker, the study concluded that the 3% that had their goals written down were earning an astounding 10 times that of the 83% group ALL PUT TOGETHER! When I heard that, I ran home and wrote down 3 goals. Grab your 3x5 card and change your life—**DO IT NOW!**

A survey published by *Fortune* magazine stated that of America's most successful executives, more than 85% of them admit to a regular regimen of goal setting.

There is also scientific evidence to back up the power of written goals. Research done by Susan Miller in 1997 indicates that our brain responds more positively when we commit our objectives to paper. It makes the goal concrete and adds to the personal commitment of achieving the goal while also adding muscle memory to the task! Miller further suggests that writing down goals, drawing them, and keeping them constantly in front of us forms a strong bond in the brain between the occipital lobe (controlling sight), the hippocampus (stored in memory), and the frontal lobe (for planning and decision making), helping the subconscious mind begin working toward goal attainment—even while we sleep!

The results are in: positive attitude, goal setting, belief, expectations, and positive visualization along with positive communication and encouragement create better students and super test takers. Start developing these characteristics **TODAY.**

CHAPTER 6

E is for
ENERGY

$\mathcal{T}$he more energy a student possesses, and the more alertness he or she exhibits, the better the student will score on tests and, in general, will be a better learner. The problem is that when taking standardized tests (including college entrance exams), the students must sit sometimes for hours without food or water. They are usually left cramped in their desks under extreme pressure exerted by the time limits of the test. Most students are not taught breathing techniques, nutritional habits or stretching exercises that would allow them to obtain the energy needed for optimum results. This chapter is dedicated to teaching those techniques that produce constant mental energy flow and alertness.

The breathing and brain gym techniques learned in Chapter 3 will definitely promote energy and can be used before and during test taking periods. The rituals and affirmation methods uncovered in Chapter 5 will also increase energy while taking a test. Use what has been working for you. If the energy yawn or calf stretch have provided positive results, then keep using them. But this book is about self-discovery and learning about multiple techniques for elevating test scores, so here are additional exercises and habits for you to develop that will insure peak performance is attained. *USE WHAT WORKS FOR YOU!*

Our first technique makes a lot of sense, but is hardly ever utilized—and that is practice! Why not? Tennis players practice their serve, ball players take batting practice, salespeople practice their sales pitch, teachers practice their presentation skills, so why shouldn't students practice their test taking skills? There is some very strong evidence that will support this theory.

David Chan and Jan Miller, in separate studies, conducted research strongly suggesting that students significantly increase their test scores when they take pre-tests or practice tests under structured conditions. They found that practice lowered the fear and anxiety associated with standardized tests and increased meaningful learning by converting information to long-term memory. It was especially helpful if the students volunteered for the practice and were motivated to take the tests.

The key to taking practice tests that produce results is in how the practice tests are administered and structured. The brain will respond the best when the practice tests are created exactly how the actual tests will be taken. For example, if the initial test segment is 45 minutes long with no breaks, recreate that scenario in the practice test. Find out what kind of chairs will be used and what the approximate temperature will be in the test room. Always practice at the exact time of day that the actual test will be taken. Will it be noisy? Will proctors be moving around the room or sitting up front? Will there be bright lights, soft lights, or sunlight? Get the picture? Recreate as much of the actual test environment as possible and then prepare for it. Use ear plugs for noise reduction, tinted glasses to reduce glare, take extra clothes if the room will be too cold for your style, and so on. **BE CREATIVE AND AGAIN—*USE WHAT WORKS FOR YOU!***

Once you make it through a practice test, your confidence will increase. You will know what to expect and be prepared for it. Preparation will avoid surprises, increase confidence, lessen nervousness, deepen the learning and provide a positive performance attitude.

Start to develop your practice test today. Use your teachers by asking them if there are already practice tests available in your school system. Schedule a practice test in a building or room set-up specifically like the testing site. Ask friends who have already taken the test what the room was like, what types of questions were asked, did anything unusual happen and any additional information needed to help you prepare. There are testing companies and web sites that can provide practice-testing conditions for you. Check them out and if they fit your style, then you might want to give them a try.

Another important item to consider is when you'll be taking your test. If it falls on the weekend of a major track meet or the day of the Prom, then see if you can change the date of the test. If not, prepare for these circumstances.

At least 5 days before the test begin to drink 8 to 12 glasses of water per day. Water is essential for thinking. The brain cannot perform in a peak manner without it. The brain has been estimated to be 85 to 90 percent water and water is the best brain fuel for peak mental performance. Our bodily systems are electrical and water is needed to keep the electrical transmissions flowing freely through our system. Water is also crucial for distributing oxygen to the brain. Water also keeps the air sacs of the lungs moist allowing for oxygen to dissolve and move through the blood. If water is not available at the testing site, take a bottle of your own and **USE IT!**

You know that oxygen is critical for the brain to operate properly and the use of breathing techniques discussed in Chapter 3 can help dramatically during a test. Studies suggest that mental stress and anxiety can rob the brain of oxygen because they disrupt the normal breathing pattern. By consciously implementing the suggested breathing techniques, the normal breathing pattern can be instantly restored or improved.

Almost all studies done on the brain indicate that aerobic conditioning is crucial for peak mental performance. When Bobby Fisher was preparing for his now famous chess matches against Boris Spasky, he developed aerobic capacity by swimming underwater for hours and lifting weights. People made jokes about his training regimen until he handily defeated Spasky, particularly during the late stages of the matches. He also made it a point to practice good posture for proper breathing techniques.

This anecdote brings up two very important points. First, it is an excellent idea to begin a walking, jogging or swimming program to build up aerobic capacity. Thirty minutes every other day is enough to develop the power needed. Second, it is important to be comfortable while taking the test. Sit in a manner compatible to your style while practicing good rules of posture. Proper posture makes breathing easier while allowing more fuel to reach the brain and lungs.

It's very important to control sleeping patterns as the test date approaches. It would be ideal if we could always practice good sleeping habits, but with the hectic schedules occupying the lives of today's youth, this is almost impossible. However, the brain does perform at a much lower level when deprived of sleep. Recent studies by J. Christian Gillin of The University of California found that lack of sleep effects the brain's ability to perform basic cognitive tasks like memorization and simple arithmetic and that overall performance is greatly diminished. This was particularly true when students "pulled an all nighter" right before the test. This evidence supports the fact that it is much better to have a good night's rest and a nutritional breakfast than it is to cram and study all night long.

During the test, it is a good idea to combine breathing *and* stretching exercises to allow the brain to "wake up". Exercises combining deep breaths while curving the spine over the back of your chair by stretching have been shown to increase the flow of cerebrospinal fluid to critical tension areas like the neck and shoulders allowing the central nervous system to relax while stimulating sensory areas like hearing and seeing.

In fact, brain states can be altered with increased energy by performing numerous exercises and also by stimulating certain areas of the body. Here are some suggestions for instant energy:

1. **THE ENERGY RUB**--The energy rub is performed by massaging the muscles around the Temporal-Mandibular Joint sometimes referred to as the TMJ. The TMJ is located just in front of the ear opening and is the joint where the lower and upper jaw come together. There are more nerve endings running across this joint than can be found anywhere else in the body, including the trunks of five major cranial nerves. When we tense up or are stressed out, our jaws tend to tighten up and the nerve activity becomes blocked causing vision problems and interfering with our ability to hear. Talking becomes a total effort and brain processing is slowed. When the mouth is opened, a hole is formed at the TMJ. This is where the gentle massaging should take place. Massage the area gently while opening and closing the jaw (See Illustration E). Try the energy rub now by massaging this area very lightly for only 20 to 30 seconds. After completion, notice how images appear much more focused and clear and how amazingly sharp the ability to hear has become. Most students also report a heightened awareness after doing this exercise. Others comment on how relaxed and alert they feel. This is a very powerful exercise to be used when performing under pressure is essential. [1]

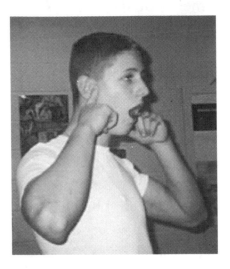

Illustration
E

2. **PAUSE FOR LAUGHTER**--Laughter forces deep breathing through the diaphragm therefore causing a relaxing effect. A good laugh also recharges the batteries and can provide a spark of instant energy. Steve Martin used to start each day by laughing at himself in a mirror for five minutes. And now science has proved that this is great therapy! Laughter aids in creativity, breaks down barriers, increases attention, and leads to a positive attitude. The next time you are feeling tense, excuse yourself, find the nearest room with a mirror and laugh away or simply laugh internally at your desk!

3. **TAKE A BREAK**--Research has proved

the validity of the theory of primacy and recency. This theory states that sharp periods of awareness and performance exist just before and after taking a break, particularly when there is a structured time period involved like taking a break every 25 minutes while studying. Studies have also shown that learning increases in proportion to the amount of breaks taken while studying. The research indicates that it would be a good idea to take breaks while studying and taking tests—stretch the legs, take deep breaths, drink some water, stand up. The break doesn't have to be long, but timing is crucial. Take the break when the attention span starts to wane. Scientists have a formula for attention span stating that our attention span (in minutes) is equal to our age plus two. So if you are 12 years old, take a break every 14 or 15 minutes. The attention span stops growing around age 28 and peaks at about 30 minutes.

4. **THE BRAIN BUTTON**--The brain button is an exercise taken from Brain Gym that provides fast, immediate energy. Drinking water before any Brain Gym exercise will increase the effectiveness of the activity. Brain Buttons are done by placing one hand over the navel while the other hand gently

rubs the indentations between the first and second ribs directly under the collarbone to the right and left of the sternum (See Illustration F). The first hand centers the body, activating the ability to focus, while the other hand stimulates blood flow through the carotid arteries to the brain. This exercise makes students more alert and brings them back to focus while taking a test.[2]

Illustration
F

5. **USE MUSIC**--Certain types of music have been shown to increase Alpha activity in the brain leading to heightened awareness and increased learning. In particular, the rhythm used in classical Baroque music effectively increases the processing of information in the brain. Something as simple as

a one-note chant has been shown to cause temporary changes in brain wave activity and states of awareness. A slow, rhythmic hum, like those used by Shamans of far eastern cultures, may be all that is needed to refocus the brain and put it back on task. Experiment and find out what rhythm and types of music are right for you.

For optimum results, adapt these strategies for what is right for your style and intelligence. Remember to keep being curious about how all these strategies will effect you and your testing abilities. Try new ideas and keep a journal about which ones work the best for you. **Go For It!**

CHAPTER 7

R is for REMEMBER

*D*id you ever study all night long and felt like you knew the material inside and out only to have your memory fail during the test? Did you ever sit at your desk knowing that you knew the answer, but just couldn't recall what it was? And as soon as you left the classroom, YOU REMEMBERED!!

In this chapter, you will discover exactly what memory is and how it works. In addition, you will be introduced to several memory enhancing techniques that will allow for deeper learning of the material and more powerful recall of the facts during testing periods. Some of these techniques can be used while studying for the test to increase retention and others can be used during the test to aid in retrieval of the information studied.

First of all, it becomes helpful if we learn exactly what memory is and how it works. The great news is that Dr. Wilder Penfield at The Montreal Neurological Institute proved that memory is permanent (hooray!). That means that we don't really forget things, but our inability to recall them becomes the problem. The problem becomes lessened when we realize that there are many ways to increase our ability to recall information depending on the type of memory being used.

That's right, there are different types of memory

and it helps to understand what they are and how to use them. Memory is usually classified in two ways. One is the life span of the memory and the second is the way in which the memory is registered and retrieved.

The first classification includes two types of memory, short-term and long-term. Short- term memory can hold onto facts for approximately 20 seconds or possibly longer if we use some of the retrieval cues explained in this chapter. This short-term memory is usually limited to seven chunks of information like remembering a phone number long enough to dial the number. Long term memory can stay with us for up to a lifetime. It is usually associated with powerful emotion and has much relevance in our lives. [1]

How information is registered and retrieved is also important. Memory can be **Explicit**, meaning it is achieved through repetition and study like spelling or multiplication tables. Memory can also be **Implicit**, meaning it happens automatically and organically like knowing that snow is cold and that the sun is hot. [2]

Implicit memory uses the body and our real life experiences to encode and retrieve information. Implicit memory has many forms that are explained in the following paragraphs.

Procedural Memory

Learning a task through repetition until it becomes automatic and requires little thinking like driving a car or tying a shoe.

Reflexive Memory

Is associated with survival. It is instant and instinctual like pulling your hand away from a hot stove. It uses intense sensory memory processes like smell, taste, and sound. Although usually unconsciously formed, there are techniques that make it possible to consciously use reflexive memory through repetition and drilling. It's important to note that any action repeated often enough can become reflexive.

Sensory Conditioning

Are the memories formed by using the different senses of the mind and body. By recreating sensory cues, memories associated with those cues can be recalled and retrieved. For instance, hearing a song played at a wedding or prom can "bring back" actual feelings and memories of the actual event. Conscious manipulation of sensory cues can also be used to trigger memory of learning that occurs during classroom or study time. We will discuss these methods later in the chapter.

Explicit Memory has many forms also. Explicit memory is associated with most of the learning tasks assigned in school and from life events. The following paragraphs explain two types of explicit memory.

Semantic Memory

Is factual memory and contains most of our knowledge from school and business. Unfortunately, semantic memory possesses the weakest of our retrieval systems.

Episodic Memory

Is activated by specific locations and circumstances. Places, faces, and events all come together to form the memory. Story telling is a powerful tool for encoding and retrieving this type of memory. [3]

Now that the basic types of memory have been defined, let's discover how to use this information to improve memory, recall, and **test scores**!

INCREASE MEMORY BY DEVELOPING THESE STUDY HABITS

1. It is very important to **RELAX BEFORE STUDYING**. You already know that the alpha brain state is best for learning and

happens during relaxation. Also, new research suggests that the hippocampus (an area
of the brain used in memory) can be adversely
effected by stress. In fact, the research indicates that brain cells within the hippocampus
can actually be destroyed under extreme
pressure! Use some of the breathing and
stretching techniques described in Chapter 3
before studying, classroom learning, or test
taking sessions.

2. It is a fact that during a learning or study
session, we remember best at the beginning of
the session and second best at the end of the
session. This proven theory is called the
primacy-recency effect and was further
strengthened by a British study conducted in
1999 by Richard Henson. This study determined that important information should be
taught at the beginning of class while attention was at a peak. Therefore, study the
difficult or important learning first and **TAKE
FREQUENT BREAKS** while learning or
studying. Every time you take a break, you
create a new beginning where learning occurs
more readily. Schedule the breaks into your
study time.

3. Divide the learning and studying into small
chunks. Arrange the learning into groups that

are related to each other and try to discover how the learning is relevant to you. What can you use this learning for? How is it important to your life? In between the learning chunks, review the material to register it even more firmly into the memory.

4. One of the most important formulas for building a super memory is learning to use Mnemonics. A book published by the U.S. Department of Education in 1989, titled **What Works**, concluded that *mnemonics allow students to remember more material and retain it longer.* Students can maximize learning in less time by using simple mnemonic tools. One example would be *Acronyms*. An Acronym is a single word made from the first letter of each word in a series. For instance, to remember the Great Lakes, use the word HOMES (Huron, Ontario, Michigan, Erie, and Superior). Another example would be *Acrostics* which also uses key words but doesn't have to be only one word or only use the first letter of the words being remembered. For instance, every musician can recall using Every Good Boy Does Fine to remember the notes on the lines in the treble clef. Using Rhymes, Jingles, Rap Songs and creative stories are also Mnemonics. They are also tremendous ways to re-

member math formulas or the conjugation of verbs in foreign language class. Research done by Foster in 1999 suggests that students who chanted and sang about material they recently learned scored significantly higher in verbal recall. Researchers also found that repetitious, rhythmic chanting reduces stress and increases relaxation, allowing the hippocampus to better store information in long-term memory. [4]

5. Eat a snack or meal high in protein, but low in calories, before studying.

6. Preview the material first, especially when studying new material or a difficult subject. Research suggests that previewing material before studying can increase learning as much as 35%!

7. Study in an area that is comfortable for you with natural lighting or lighting that suits your learning style.

8. Making the learning active will help concentration and increase recall. So highlight key facts using different colors, ask yourself questions, take notes, and self-test on what you have learned.

9. Practice reading material out loud to activate more areas of the brain. If you are an auditory learner, use an accent while you read and alternate reading loud and soft or fast and slow. If you are a visual, hook up mental pictures to the learning. Use your individual style to enhance memory.

10. The more unusual or humorous the learning is, the more easily it is remembered. Associate learning with events or stories that are funny or unique and unusual.

Two of the most important techniques for developing a super memory are:
- Review often.
- Make sure that you get enough sleep.

You may wonder what sleep has to do with having a good memory, but new research suggests that memory can be significantly impaired by lack of adequate rest. The research indicates that cramming all night for a test is counterproductive and the student would be better off by simply reviewing the material, then going to bed and getting a good night's rest. Some researchers have uncovered amazing data about the dream state or REM (rapid eye movement) state of sleep. Studies indicate that the last few hours of sleep in the morning (high REM state) are critical for memory formation of the previous day's learning. The rule of thumb is that the more complex and complicated the learning, then the more important sleep is to transferring the material to long-term memory. Student control groups were tested in the afternoon of the same day over material learned during morning classes and scored 9%. Other students were taught the identical material, but allowed to get a full night's rest before being tested the next day. They scored an amazing 56%! In other words, learning increased six times by simply getting enough rest in between the learning and the testing!!!

This research would suggest the following additions to our study strategies. First, avoid any outside distractions that wake you up in the early morning hours like the dog barking, the paper arriving, or setting the alarm clock too early. If this can't be done, **GO TO BED EARLIER!!** Secondly, a very powerful method to increase memory is to review the material before going to sleep, then sleep and let the brain process the learning into long-term memory. If time allows, add the third step of reviewing the material again in the morning upon awakening.

Which brings us to review. Without review, memory drops out of our consciousness. It's simple, the more you review something, the more it sticks in your mind. The average person forgets 70% of what they learn within 24 hours, but the following simple process will allow you to remember 80% of what you learn after 6 months!! Try this:

1. Learn the material
2. Review it briefly after one hour
3. Review it once more after one day
4. Review it again after one week
5. Review it again after one month
6. Review it again after six months

During these review sessions only review highlighted or important material. Each review should only take 4-6 minutes. Therefore, ° hour of review over 6 months time will result in tripling your memory! Don't take my word for it—**TRY IT!**[5]

Another common sense method for improving memory is learning how to take good notes. It has long been thought that good note taking can increase learning and now the research is available to prove that short-term and long-term memory are improved by practicing good note taking skills. Writing notes also activates more neural pathways for better recall of the learning while allowing the brain to organize the information and make sense of complicated material. A helpful tip to remember is that shorter, more concise note taking helps the brain digest information better than long, rambling notes. Also, having the notes available for review greatly facilitates recall and aids the brain in storing material into long-term memory.

There are basically 4 steps to memory:

1. Learn and review the material.
2. Encode the material—putting the information into long-term memory.
3. Maintenance of the material—rein forcing memory, being able to hold onto memory for long periods of time.
4. Retrieval of the information—being able to remember the information when needed.

If we can learn more powerful ways to encode material into long-term memory, then the memories will last longer and be easier to recall during testing sessions.

STRATEGIES FOR POWERFUL ENCODING OF IN-FORMATION

1. Draw pictures of what the learning means to your personally. Visualize yourself using the new learning in your personal life. Add vivid colors and brightness to your drawings and visualizations.
2. Over learn the material. Pretend like you are the teacher and make a lesson plan for teach-

ing the material to someone else. Better still would be to set aside some time each evening to make a lesson plan and teach your parents or siblings the new information. Teaching something to other learners deeply roots the material into long-term memory.

3. Develop a positive attitude about learning. Decide that you will remember the information. As you learned earlier, positive attitude can alter the chemistry of the brain, releasing neurotransmitters that help in learning and memory. Use "I am" statements for fostering belief—"I am a good learner", "I am a good test-taker", "I possess a great memory".

4. Use music, rhythm, and rhyming to solidify learning. Create raps, rhymes, and songs for putting the learning into music. Using music allows for more permanent encoding into long-term memory.

5. Engage emotion. The more emotion involved in the learning, the deeper the learning is encoded into memory. Use techniques like role-playing, cheers, singing, stretching, field trips, debates, and personal stories to supply positive emotions to learning. Be creative and invent ways to stir up emotion using your personal learning style.

The more of our senses we involve in the emotion, the more neural pathways are created for learning and memory. Therefore, make learning activities and environments sensory rich for the best results.

Of all the senses, smell seems to the one that humans can best use for increasing learning and memory. For instance, studies done by Dr. Alan Hirsch, a Chicago neurologist, indicate that floral odors increase the ability to learn, create and think. His research revealed that when smelling floral odors, the subjects of his study were able to solve problems and puzzles 30% faster! This would suggest that when taking a math or science test, it would help to smell a carnation or rose when confronted with puzzles or mathematical problems.

Research would also suggest that **peppermint, lemon,** and **cinnamon** are the best scents for anchoring learning into the brain. I have worked with students that swear by this method. They study English in a room filled with peppermint odor, obtained through a spray, candle, or food flavoring. They might study math in a room that smells like lemon. But when they are tested in English, they eat a peppermint lifesaver and when tested in math, they suck on a lemon hard candy. The memories of what they studied in the rooms begin flowing into the brain helping them to answer the most difficult questions! **It's worth a try**. The smell of lemons also helps to improve focus and concentration and may be used before a study session or before taking a test.

Smells can also regulate stress by lowering anxiety and producing a relaxed emotional state. To **reduce stress, use vanilla, lavender, rose, or jasmine.** To **energize yourself, use peppermint, rosemary, or thyme.** Lemon or mint can be used as background aromas to increase alertness and boost productivity.

Some of these scents can be used in the flavoring of tea. This would be a great alternative to drinking sodas or coffee before a learning experience. **It can't hurt to give this a try!**

INSTANT MEMORY TIP:

There is an exercise called The Thinking Cap that comes from Brain Gym and can improve hearing and memory almost instantly. It works because of the strong correlation between hearing in the temporal lobe and memory in the limbic system. The next time you have an answer on the tip of your tongue or when you are struggling to remember something that you know, use your fingers to "unroll" the outer part of your ears from top to bottom several times. Hearing will instantly become more acute and the chances of remembering information dramatically increase. **TRY THIS EXERCISE AND AMAZE YOURSELF!!** [6]

That's it! The **DRIVER TECHNIQUE** for achieving higher exam scores. The neat thing is you don't have to do all the elements in the technique. Start small and work on one thing at a time. Discover what works for you and stick with it. You could discover that by using only one area of the **DRIVER TECHNIQUE**, your test scores begin to skyrocket!

In the next two chapters, we'll discover how to use all the knowledge we've learned thus far to design and arrange our personal learning environment. To build our own personal study room! Then we'll learn how to use our new information while preparing for a test and then while actually taking the test. **LET'S GO!!**

CHAPTER 8

Creating A Super
Learning Environment

In the following pages, you will learn how to design and build a *personal* learning environment. Your learning room will reflect your preferred learning style and take full advantage of your personal intelligences. The object is to have a learning environment available to you that will allow you to get the most possible out of your study time. This means you will have to discover the many ways in which you learn the best. You can do this by experimenting (use techniques in Chapter 4), trial and error, or by taking the Dunn, Dunn & Price Personal Learning Inventory supplied by your guidance counselor.

Currently, there is much research to support the value of an enriched learning environment. These environments stimulate growth of neural connections, helping to develop new synapses while strengthening existing ones, and produce better learners. Let's explore this research and discover suggestions on how to create such an environment.

First of all, what color should our room be?

The power of color is frequently underestimated. Most of the research done concerning color would indicate that the best learning environments would contain the colors **blue** or **green** for a calming effect while **yellow, beige** or **off-white** would be best for optimal learning. A combination of these colors may be the best for learning and retaining information. Experiment to see what's best for you.

Hayden Frye, the football coach at the University of Iowa, had a tremendous string of games won at home. He attributes part of his success to the colors of the home and visiting teams' locker rooms. The Iowa locker room is blue supporting feelings of strength and aggression. The visitors locker room is pink causing a weakening of muscle strength. [1]

A very interesting study was done in 1979 at the University of California within the state prison system. Prison guards were asked to do arm curl exercises with heavy dumbbells. Most of them averaged 28 curls before tiring and having to stop. After doing the curls, a tall, wide, blue poster board was held in front of the guards and they were asked to repeat the exercise. Without much rest in-between they were able to duplicate and often surpass their previous results. However, they were then put in front of a tall, wide pink poster and asked to repeat the exercise. Even after being allowed to rest, most could only perform 5 or 6 curls! [2]

The colors **blue, green,** and **brown** have the

same effect on the human mind. They seem to generate a calming effect and produce an optimal learning state. There have been studies done about the color of paper used for tests and these studies suggest that test scores improve when the test is given on blue or green paper!

Put positive posters on the walls throughout the room. We already know that the more positive the environment, the more learning occurs. Use motivational posters, beautiful scenery, framed classroom work, and forms of personal expression. When using these materials, always remember to display them above eye level so the learner has to activate the visual cortex by looking up at the material. This simple suggestion allows more of the positive message and beauty of the posters to reach crucial areas of the brain.

The lighting in the room is very important.

Some learners like bright lights and others prefer dimly lit environments. Discover what you prefer and decorate accordingly. Most research suggests that the worst type of lighting for the room would be fluorescent lighting, so avoid fluorescent lighting at all costs. Low-moderate level lighting seems to be the best for most students, but the ideal lighting is indirect natural sunlight. If sunlight is not an option, there is a brand of light bulb produced called Vitalite. Vitalite produces full spectrum lighting and research indicates it can improve the immune system as well as enhance learning and memory.

During the darker winter months, increase the brightness of the lighting. If the learner is hyper and excited, dim the lights for study. If he or she is too relaxed or becomes sleepy, then increase the amount of lighting. It would be ideal to have a dimmer switch for our learning room.

What about the air in the room?

This factor is constantly overlooked, but the effects upon learning and memory can be substantial. Overexposure to air pollutants is known to effect memory, growth, attention span, and reading skills by interfering with the brain's transmission of certain neurotransmitters. There are air purifiers produced on the market that can help lower the amount of pollutants in our learning room.

Research also suggests that learning can be impaired by highly electrified air. The normal atmosphere contains a healthy balance of positive and negative ions. Human activity and pollutants can destroy negative ions in the air we breathe causing depression and sleepiness. Negative air is best for learning and there are devices called "environmental ionizers" that can healthfully balance the electrical charge of the air in our learning room. They are relatively inexpensive, but the benefits are outstanding. Negative air has been shown to improve the performance of the immune system while increasing alertness and attention in learners. To save yourself money when building your learning room, purchase an air purifier that also ionizes the air. [3]

Should the room be soundproofed?

That depends on the learner. Noise distractions can disrupt mental focus in some students. It's a good idea that when learning new material, the environment should contain as few distractions as possible. Most research still indicates that the brain performs best when attention is focused. However, some students learn best in a noisy, busy environment. The use of earplugs to control the noise level would be an option if soundproofing is unavailable or not in the budget. Discover how you learn the best and design your learning room appropriately.

Equip the learning room with a sound system. This sound system should allow for the use of a headset and be equipped to play CDs or tapes. The research on music strongly suggests that playing the correct type of music will increase learning and boost memory and recall. Music can also speed healing, promote relaxation, enhance learning and arouse emotions.

Most research suggests that Baroque classical, New Age, and even some Jazz can be used to enhance learning. During the studies, music fostered creativity and stimulated imagination while also changing the energy states of the subjects. Certain types of music may be better for different applications. For instance, Lazanov's research would suggest that classical and romantic music is best for introducing new information, while Baroque music may be best for reviewing subject matter.

There is way too much information available on music and its effect on learning to be covered in this chapter. However, you can learn all you need to know by reading these books: **Music with the Brain in Mind** by Eric Jensen and **The Mozart Effect** by Don Campbell. These books will provide you with interesting reading material and solidify the conclusion that any learning environment should be equipped with a sound system to provide music to the learner. These resources will also provide many creative ways to use music for motivation, relaxation, memory, and learning.

The learning environment should be equipped with means to control climate.

Heaters, air conditioners, humidifiers and air purifiers are important because temperature and air density can effect learning. Some students work best when they are hot, others like the cold. Find out your preference and design the room accordingly. Research suggests that choosing temperature may be the most important choice students may make in regulating their environment. Comfortable temperatures are dependent upon age, gender, time of day and other miscellaneous factors. Therefore, comfort is relative to each individual.

However, there are some generalities suggested in the research. Warmer temps can arouse the learner and colder temps can relax the learner, making them more receptive. Research would indicate that a moderate temperature range is best for alertness. If temperatures become too high, try breathing air through the nose. This technique has been discovered to cool the brain and aid in relaxation. [4]

The type of furniture selection depends on the learning style of the student.

Most students will learn better if seated in

ergonomically correct furniture. Research by Dunn and Dunn suggests that students need choices in posture and seating to learn effectively. Some students can use the floor while others prefer bean-bag chairs. Still others want hard-backed chairs and others like pillows. Make the choice based upon self-discovery and what works best for the individual.

The learning room should come equipped with scented sprays, scented candles, scented oils, incense, and certain flavored hard candies.

We know that recall can be easier when using scents like peppermint, lemon, and cinnamon. We also know that stimulating the olfactory system can help in problem solving. Take advantage of this knowledge and create a room with aromas that make the learner feel comfortable and confident. Provide odors and aromas that can aid in long term memory by providing the learner with a sensory cue for vivid recall.

Finally, each learning room should have an aquarium and plenty of plants.

The water sounds of the aquarium provide relaxation while the esthetic benefits of colorful fish and surroundings help to enrich the environment. The National Space and Aeronautics Administration has discovered that plants provide a super environment for scientific thinking and learning. Studies have proved that plants can affect an area of 100 square feet by raising the oxygen level in the air while removing air pollutants and increasing the air's negative ionization. [6]

There you have it—some super suggestions on designing and building a learning environment. **BUILD ONE TODAY** and watch those test scores rise!

CHAPTER 9

Taking the Test

This chapter provides a mental and physical checklist filled with reminders about what a student can do the day before the test and while taking the test to improve performance.

The days before the test are important and can be used to prepare the brain and the body for the event. Here are some tips that will help you prepare in the days and nights before the test.

1. Begin to watch your diet three to five days before the test. Avoid food colorings and additives like MSG and aspartame. Drink plenty of water and start to develop a surplus for the brain to use during the test.
2. Start planting sensory cues to be used for recall during the test by associating scents, temperatures, and music to the learning. Use different aromas for different subjects. Use different songs or types of music for each subject. Create jingles, raps and acronyms to help you remember during test time.
3. Get plenty of sleep. It will help you be more alert and aid in the formation of memory.
4. Use affirmation training as the test approaches. Tell yourself you are capable and believe you will do well on the test. Use "I am" statements to boost confidence.
5. See yourself doing well on the test. When visualizing, see the room as it will be ar-

ranged and feel the temperature. See yourself performing well and answering all questions to the best of your ability. Picture a
smile on your face as you sit confidently
finishing the test. Remember to visualize
with vivid colors and to see the mental re-
hearsal sharp, up close, and focused.
6. Review for the test the night before just
   before going to bed to allow your subconscious to work on the answers all night long.
7. When you wake up the morning of the test,
   start the day by telling yourself that you are
   looking forward to taking the test and that
   it's going to be a super day.

And now the test is here! Let's use what we
have learned to help us relax and have a super
memory during the test. You may decide to make a
checklist of the following reminders and take the
list to the test with you. Use these techniques and
you'll be surprised at how much you remember and
how good you feel about being tested on the material.

1. Take a bottle of water with you to the test.
2. Remember to take scented candies or oils
   to the testing room. Use the scents that
   you have hooked up memories and learning to. Suck the candies when you need to
   recall that specific learning. You can also

rub the scented oils on your wrists and smell them when you are stumped on a question.

3. Have a protein snack 15 to 20 minutes before the test to help you remain alert.

4. Visualize the color blue, green or beige. It worked for the weightlifters— it will work for you.

5. Use relaxation techniques by taking deep breaths and stretching the muscles. Pay particular attention to the TMJ and calf muscles. Review (Chapter 3) on relaxation and use the information.

6. Skim the test and answer the questions that you know as you go along. Read the questions you aren't sure of and think about the answers while you are skimming the test. Go through the test again—some of the answers will have come to you automatically. The third time you go through the test use your memory techniques to help you answer the difficult questions. For instance, think of what the room was like when you learned the material. Was it hot? Cold? Where were you sitting? Try to remember where the teacher was standing when she taught the material or if she used any special techniques like role playing, cheers, or games to teach you the information. If you used

a song or scent to anchor the learning, then start playing the song in your head or suck on a candy containing the scent (peppermint, lemon) that the learning is hooked up to. [1]

7. Remember to rub the outside of the ears in a rolling motion to stimulate memory (the thinking cap from Brain Gym).

8. Take a floral scent to the room and use it for additional help in solving problems or puzzles that may be on the test.

9. Make sure you have a supply of tissues. Remember, the clearer your nasal passages are, the better you'll perform. Use a breathe right strip if you have to—**whatever it takes!!**

10.Take stretching breaks during the test. Lean back over the chair and stretch as far as you can. Wake up the brain!

11.When doing math problems, doodle with the right hand to activate the left hemisphere of the brain. When being creative, do exercises with the left hand to activate the right hemisphere of the brain.

12.If you are having trouble remembering a specific answer, try and remember something related to that question. Chances are the answer will come to you.

13.Reread the test and look for silly mistakes.

Walk to the front of the room, hand in your test and tell yourself what a great job you did!

Review this book often. It is filled with information that can help you and your friends avoid the stress of taking standardized tests. These techniques will also help you in sports, professional development, job interviews, relationships, and almost anything!

You are a genius! Be confident! Go for it! And please let me know if I can ever help.

GOOD LUCK!!!

RESOURCES

1: The D.R.I.V.E.R System

[1] Hills, Sandra, N.D. and Wyman, Pat, M.A. *What's Food got to do with it?* Windsor, CA: The Center for New Discoveries in Learning, 1997. P. 156

2: D is for DIET (NUTRITION)

[1] Wurtman, Judith J. PH.D. *Managing Your Mind & Mood Through Food.* New York: Harper & Row, 1988. pp. 18-22

[2] Wurtman, Judith J. PH.D. *Managing Your Mind & Mood Through Food.* New York: Harper & Row, 1988. pp. 18-22

[3] Jensen, Eric. *The Learning Brain.* San Diego: Turning Point Publishing, 1995. p.151

[4] Wurtman, Judith J. PH.D. *Managing Your Mind & Mood Through Food.* New York: Harper & Row, 1988. p.64

[5] Hills, Sandra, N.D. and Wyman, Pat, M.A. *What's Food got to do with it?* Windsor, CA: The Center for New Discoveries in Learning, 1997. pp.12-14

[6] Hills, Sandra, N.D. and Wyman, Pat, M.A. *What's Food got to do with it?* Windsor, CA: The Center for New Discoveries in Learning, 1997. pp. 12-14

[7] Hills, Sandra, N.D. and Wyman, Pat, M.A. *What's Food got to do with it?* Windsor, CA: The Center for New Dis-

coveries in Learning, 1997. pp. 12-14

8 Markowitz, M.A., Karen, and Jensen, M.A., Eric. *The Great Memory Book.* San Diego, CA: The Brain Store, 1999. pp. 122-123

3: R is for RELAXATION

1 Kenyon, Tom. *Brain States.* Naples, FL: United States Publishing, 1994. pp. 37-38

2 Kenyon, Tom. *Brain States.* Naples, FL: United States Publishing, 1994. pp.40-41

3 Kenyon, Tom. *Brain States.* Naples, FL: United States Publishing, 1994. p.40

4 Loehr, Dr. James E. and McLaughlin, Peter J. *Mentally Tough.* New York: M. Evans and Company, Inc., 1986. p. 140

5 Loehr, Dr. James E. and McLaughlin, Peter J. *Mentally Tough.* New York: M. Evans and Company, Inc., 1986 p. 142.

6 Loehr, Dr. James E. and McLaughlin, Peter J. *Mentally Tough.* New York: M. Evans and Company, Inc., 1986. p. 143

7 Loehr, Dr. James E. and McLaughlin, Peter J. *Mentally Tough.* New York: M. Evans and Company, Inc., 1986. p. 144

8 Loehr, Dr. James E. and McLaughlin, Peter J. *Mentally Tough.* New York: M. Evans and Company,

Inc., 1986. pp. 144-145

9 Hannaford, Carla. *Smart Moves*. Arlington, Virginia: Great Ocean Publishing, 1995. p. 167

10 Hannaford, Carla. *Smart Moves*. Arlington, Virginia: Great Ocean Publishing, 1995. p. 128

11 Hannaford, Carla. *Smart Moves*. Arlington, Virginia: Great Ocean Publishing, 1995. p. 121

12 Hannaford, Carla. *Smart Moves*. Arlington, Virginia: Great Ocean Publishing, 1995. p. 119

13 Kenyon, Tom. *Brain States*. Naples, FL: United States Publishing, 1994. pp. 78-79

4: I is for INDIVIDUALITY

1 Chapman, Carolyn. *If The Shoe FITS...* Arlington Heights, IL: IRI/SkyLight Training and Publishing, 1993. p. 23

2 Chapman, Carolyn. *If The Shoe FITS...* Arlington Heights, IL: IRI/SkyLight Training and Publishing, 1993. p. 55

3 Chapman, Carolyn. *If The Shoe FITS...* Arlington Heights, IL: IRI/SkyLight Training and Publishing, 1993. p. 81

4 Chapman, Carolyn. *If The Shoe FITS...* Arlington Heights, IL: IRI/SkyLight Training and Publishing, 1993. p. 107

[5] Chapman, Carolyn. *If The Shoe FITS...* Arlington Heights, IL: IRI/SkyLight Training and Publishing, 1993. p. 133

[6] Chapman, Carolyn. *If The Shoe FITS...* Arlington Heights, IL: IRI/SkyLight Training and Publishing, 1993. p. 153

[7] Chapman, Carolyn. *If The Shoe FITS...* Arlington Heights, IL: IRI/SkyLight Training and Publishing, 1993. p. 171

[8] Chapman, Carolyn. *If The Shoe FITS...* Arlington Heights, IL: IRI/SkyLight Training and Publishing, 1993. p. 195

[9] Wurtman, Judith J. PH.D. *Managing Your Mind & Mood Through Food.* New York: Harper & Row, 1988. Activator, pp. 5-11

[10] Wurtman, Judith J. PH.D. *Managing Your Mind & Mood Through Food.* New York: Harper & Row, 1988. Activator, pp. 12-20

[11] Wurtman, Judith J. PH.D. *Managing Your Mind & Mood Through Food.* New York: Harper & Row, 1988. Activator, pp. 21-22

[12] Wurtman, Judith J. PH.D. *Managing Your Mind & Mood Through Food.* New York: Harper & Row, 1988. Activator, pp. 23-25

[13] Wurtman, Judith J. PH.D. *Managing Your Mind & Mood Through Food.* New York: Harper & Row, 1988. Activator, pp. 26-31

[14] Johnson, Kerry J. *Sales Magic.* New York: William Morrow & Company, Inc., 1994. p. 30

5: V is for VISUALIZING CONFIDENCE

[1] Kassner, Kimberly. *You're a Genius and I Can Prove It.* Mill Valley, CA.: EmpowerMind, 1996. pp. 114-115

6: E is for ENERGY STATE

1 Hannaford, Carla. *Smart Moves.* Arlington, Virginia: Great Ocean Publishing, 1995. p. 126

2 Hannaford, Carla. *Smart Moves.* Arlington, Virginia: Great Ocean Publishing, 1995. p. 117

7: R is for REMEMBER

[1] Markowitz, M.A., Karen, and Jensen, M.A., Eric. *The Great Memory Book.* San Diego, CA: The Brain Store, 1999. p. 2

[2] Markowitz, M.A., Karen, and Jensen, M.A., Eric. *The Great Memory Book.* San Diego, CA: The Brain Store, 1999. pp. 2-3

[3] Markowitz, M.A., Karen, and Jensen, M.A., Eric. *The Great Memory Book.* San Diego, CA: The Brain Store, 1999. pp. 3-5

[4] Markowitz, M.A., Karen, and Jensen, M.A., Eric. *The Great Memory Book.* San Diego, CA: The Brain Store, 1999. p. 62

5 Tracy, Brian. *Accelerated Learning Techniques*. Niles,
IL: Nightengale Conant, 1995 –
casssette tape program. Tape 5

6 Hannaford, Carla. *Smart Moves*. Arlington, Virginia:
Great Ocean Publishing, 1995. pp. 125-126

8: Creating A Super Learning Environment

1 Walker, Dr. Morton. *The Power of Color*. New York:
Avery Publishing Group, Inc., 1991
by Morton Walker. p. 43

2 Walker, Dr. Morton. *The Power of Color*. New York:
Avery Publishing Group, Inc., 1991
by Morton Walker. p. 44

3 Jensen, Eric. *The Learning Brain*. San Diego:
Turning Point Publishing, 1995. p. 307

4 Jensen, Eric. *The Learning Brain*. San Diego:
Turning Point Publishing, 1995. p. 311

5 Jensen, Eric. *The Learning Brain*. San Diego:
Turning Point Publishing, 1995. p. 314

9: Taking The Test

1 Kassner, Kimberly. *You're a Genius and I Can Prove It.*
Mill Valley, CA.: EmpowerMind, 1996. p. 102

Bibliography

Campbell, Don. *The Mozart Effect*. New York: Avon Books, 1997.

Chapman, Carolyn. *If The Shoe FITS...* Arlington Heights, IL: IRI/SkyLight Training and Publishing, 1993.

Dunn, Kenneth J., Ed.D. *Amazing Grades*. Arlington, VA: Learning Matters, Inc., 1991.

Hannaford, Carla. *Smart Moves*. Arlington, Virginia: Great Ocean Publishing, 1995.

Hills, Sandra, N.D. and Wyman, Pat, M.A. *What's Food got to do with it?* Windsor, CA: The Center for New Discoveries in Learning, 1997.

Jensen, Eric. *The Learning Brain*. San Diego: Turning Point Publishing, 1995.

Jensen, Eric. *Music with the Brain in Mind*. San Diego: The Brain Store, Inc., 2000.

Johnson, Kerry J. *Sales Magic*. New York: William Morrow & Company, Inc., 1994.

Kassner, Kimberly. *You're a Genius and I Can Prove It*. Mill Valley, CA.: EmpowerMind, 1996.

Kenyon, Tom. *Brain States*. Naples, FL: United States Publishing, 1994.

Kline, Peter, and Martel, Laurence D. *School Success.*
Atlanta, GA: Great Ocean Publishing, 1992 by Learning
Matters, Inc.

Loehr, Dr. James E. and McLaughlin, Peter J. *Mentally Tough.*
New York: M. Evans and Company, Inc., 1986.

Markowitz, M.A., Karen, and Jensen, M.A., Eric.
The Great Memory Book. San Diego, CA: The Brain Store,
1999.

Tracy, Brian. *Accelerated Learning Techniques.* Niles, IL:
Nightengale Conant, 1995 – casssette tape program.

Walker, Dr. Morton. *The Power of Color.* New York:
Avery Publishing Group, Inc., 1991 by Morton Walker.

Wurtman, Judith J. PH.D. *Managing Your Mind & Mood
Through Food.* New York: Harper & Row, 1988.

THE AUTHOR

Bruce Boguski is an author, motivational speaker, columnist, and media personality well known for his ability to inspire others to "do the impossible". Bruce holds a   B.S. degree in business and education from Bowling Green State University. He also possesses a Level Two Certification in Brain Based Learning Strategies.

Bruce knows first hand the attitude and skills required to overcome physical and mental challenges. At age 18, Bruce was partially paralyzed in an automobile accident. Although doctors warned that he might never walk again, he left the hospital a few months later under his own power. After a two-year struggle to regain full use of his body, Bruce went on to become a two-time state champion in Racquetball and played on a state championship softball team. He later served as head baseball coach and assistant football coach at Van Buren High School and the men's and women's tennis coach at The University of Findlay.

Today, Bruce is President of The Winner's Edge, a peak performance consulting firm in Findlay, Ohio where he resides with his wife, Mary and two children, Brian and Allison. He is a nationally known presenter on motivational tactics and mental toughness training for school, sports, and business, using high-energy, interactive techniques to inspire and delight his audiences.

Bruce loves speaking to educators, parents, students,

159

athletes, and business professionals and has conducted over 1700 presentations in the past 10 years. Some of his topics include:

- **Finding the "Zone"** - Developing the ability to perform under pressure in a peak manner in sales, sports and school.
- **The Learning Zone** - Discovering secrets for relaxation, increased learning, and super memory.
- **The Golf Zone** - Use these mental strategies to cut 2 to 6 strokes off your score immediately.
- **The Testing Zone** - Helping students develop strategies to handle the stress associated with standardized tests.
- **Going For Your Dreams** - A step by step blueprint for turning dreams into reality.

Along with seminars on teamwork, stress reduction, self esteem, and motivation.

If you would like more information about seminars or products by The Winner's Edge call (419) 424-3910

The Winner's Edge
6924 Township Road 136
Findlay, Ohio 45840
(419) 424-3910
www.thewinnersedge.cc

Additional Products by the Author

Give yourself a tremendous advantage by learning the mental skills required to play consistent golf. Casual and Professional golfers will admit golf is almost 100% mental. With this extraordinary product get a head start on your season, using mental toughness training techniques to improve your game almost overnight.
This product contains 2 audiocassettes and a workbook sharing techniques used by star athletes to improve the mental game of golf.

A dynamic and insightful look at the quest for achieving your dreams. You will learn the biggest reason people do not reach for their dreams and how to overcome this obstacle. Master the ability to change your positive attitude into positive belief. Discover how time can actually become your ally and the attribute we all possess but seldom use. Determine the one word you never use when pursuing a dream. Available in cassette or CD.

There is a word that can strike fear into the heart of the mightiest athlete, cause panic in the most determined performer, and baffle the most knowledgeable coaches. The word is *"Slump"*. Learn why slumps start, how to prevent them. This product reveals the secrets to end slumps in sports, business, and education. Contains cassette and workbook.

Notes:

Notes:

Notes:

Notes:

Notes:

Notes: